US AIRCREW
COMBAT FLIGHT &
SURVIVAL GEAR

Dedication
For my brother Piet

Acknowledgements
I am grateful for the generous support of many people over the years - and first, to the ALSE techs who issued and maintained my flight gear in Vietnam and since; they are a professional little crew of unsung heroes, and I would like to thank them all. I would like to salute specifically two of the ALSE congregation: Sgt.Debbie Gifford and Sgt.Steven Robertson from Company G, 140th Aviation Regiment (Delta Schooners); they not only issue and maintain the gear for their extremely active National Guard unit, they are regular crew members on my beloved old CH-47 Chinooks - still flying after thirty years of service.

Rick Stewart at SOS Survival Life Support, a company supplying survival equipment frequently used by military aircrew, provided excellent information and gave access to some products for photography. Some of the equipment in this book is available from that company: SOS Survival Life Support, N 3808 Sullivan Road Bldg.6, Spokane Industrial Park, Spokane, Washington USA 99216, phone (509) 927-7006. George Hedges and Leo Unruh from the Gentex Corporation also generously provided much information about their amazing product line and development program.

Capt.John Cotter and MSgt.Joseph De Simas III at the 144th Fighter Wing provided tremendous help with many aspects of the project, and John not only baby-sat us but modelled the latest in USAF fashion. Sgt.Tim Williams from the 129th Air National Guard took the initiative to ensure that the legendary USAF para-rescue ("PJ") crews, with their exotic missions and gear, were part of the story. And a small squadron of advisors and models from the US Coast Guard's Air Station San Francisco - Fred Fijn in particular - demonstrated the Guard's versions of the gear. Finally, thanks to the USAF, US Army, US Coast Guard, and US Marine Corps for their hospitality on many occasions over the past few years. They have permitted me - an elderly, decrepit relic of another era - to fly aboard (and sometimes operate) a wide variety of military combat and transport aircraft.

Hans Halberstadt
San Jose
July 1995

Stock Photography
Most of photographs in this book are available as stock images through Arms Communications, 1517 Maurice Drive, Woodbridge, Virginia USA 22191, phone (703) 690-3338.

US AIRCREW COMBAT FLIGHT & SURVIVAL GEAR

Photographs by HANS & MIKE HALBERSTADT

Text by HANS HALBERSTADT

Motorbooks International
Publishers & Wholesalers ®

This edition first published in 1996 by
Motorbooks International Publishers
& Wholesalers, 729 Prospect Avenue,
PO Box 1, Osceola, WI 54020 USA

© Hans & Mike Halberstadt

Previously published in Great Britain by
Windrow & Greene Ltd.
5 Gerrard Street, London W1V 7LJ

Motorbooks International is a certified trademark,
registered with the United States Patent Office.

The information in this book is true and complete to the
best of our knowledge. All recommendations are made
without any guarantee on the part of the author or
publisher, who also disclaim any liability incurred in
connection with the use of this data or specific details.

We recognize that some words, model names and
designations, for example, mentioned herein are the
property of the trademark holder. We use them for
identification purposes only. This is not an official
publication.

Motorbooks International books are also available at
discounts in bulk quantity for industrial or sales-
promotional use. For details write to Special Sales
Manager at the Publisher's address.

Library of Congress Cataloging-in-Publication Data
Available.

ISBN 0-7603-0267-7

Printed and bound in Hong Kong

CONTENTS

CHAPTER 1
Basher Five Two

riday 2 June 1995: "Basher" Flight - a pair of US Air Force F-16 Fighting Falcons - is patrolling at 26,000 feet above the Bosnian province of what had once been the federated Republic of Yugoslavia, and is now a chaotic jigsaw puzzle of enclaves and killing zones contested by at least seven separate regular and irregular armies. So far combat aircraft have played little part in the bloodletting; but there have been isolated sneak attacks by elderly MiGs, retained by the Serbian and Croatian regimes on former Yugoslav Air Force bases, and the United Nations have declared the skies over Bosnia-Herzogovina a "no-fly" zone in an attempt to limit, however slightly, the warring parties' potential for slaughter. Today the flight leader is Captain Bob Wright, his wingman Captain Scott O'Grady, both from the USAF's 555th Tactical Fighter Squadron operating out of Aviano, Italy.

Suddenly the tedium of an uneventful patrol is broken: the RAW (radar attack warning) scopes light up in both aircraft. Somewhere below the unbroken

(**Above & left**) An F-16 Fighting Falcon in today's low-visibility finish of subdued grays, in this case an aircraft of the 144th Fighter Wing; and the 144th's Lieutenant-Colonel Bill Gore, wearing the "fast slacks" from the Combat Edge outfit over his CWU-27/P flight suit, and carrying the Combat Edge helmet.

Captain John Cotter, the 144th Fighter Wing's genial Executive Support Officer, models complete basic day wear for the well-dressed F-16 pilot: parachute harness, over survival vest, over life preserver, over anti-G pants, over Nomex flight suit. His survival vest is set up differently from those used by Navy, Marine and Army fliers - many "local" variations on the basic design will be found throughout the photographs in this book.

(Left) If you have to eject in unfriendly territory, then once you're safely on the ground and have shed your 'chute harness, grab the two little rucksack-type packs of the ejection seat survival kit before you make a break for the underbrush. These two bags are loaded with tools and supplies which can save your hide under a wide range of conditions - assuming you stayed awake during survival classes.

(Right) LTC Bill Gore inserting himself into the cockpit of his F-16; the parachute harness will be clipped to the 'chute stowage of his ejection seat and fastened before take-off.

(Right & overleaf) Down in the weeds, and perhaps on the run from unfriendlies, your best way home is through the trusty PRC-90 radio. They usually give you two (one in the seat kit, one in your survival vest), presumably reasoning that the average aviator will inevitably manage to lose one of them in the process of departing from the cockpit - the only place where he can be trusted to function efficiently.

cloud cover - and much to the surprise of Basher Flight and the whole NATO air component - a pair of Serbian SA-6 mobile surface-to-air (SAM) missile launchers energize their systems; track the F-16s; lock on - and launch. The missiles streak into the overcast sky, accelerating quickly to the speed of sound and beyond, arcing upward in a trajectory calculated to intercept the targets four miles above the ground. In the cockpits of both fighters the RAW displays the progress of the missiles; an ominous warning tone sounds in the headsets of both pilots; but the cloud cover prevents either from seeing the missiles and evading effectively.

The first missile splits the difference between the two F-16s; its warhead explodes between them without damaging either of the fighters. But the second SAM homes in relentlessly on Basher Five Two, streaking out of the top of the grey cloud to detonate squarely under Capt.O'Grady's aircraft. All the flight leader sees is the flash from the warhead - then his wingman's

airframe breaks in half just astern of the cockpit. The sleek F-16 disintegrates before his eyes, transformed into a tumbling mass of flaming wreckage which disappears into the cloud. In a shockingly brief moment Basher Flight leader finds himself alone in the sky.

Captain O'Grady has a different perspective: he feels a jolt, hears a bang - then watches his warm, cosy little world come apart. Fire engulfs the cockpit. The instrument panel of the F-16 warps and shatters before his eyes. It is obviously time to depart the aircraft. This is a moment the crews of "fast-movers" think about often, and pray never comes; you train for it, try to condition your mind for this instant, try to be prepared for the simple, extreme performance required to eject from an airplane. And now it has arrived for Scott O'Grady. He releases the useless throttle and control column, reaches down between his thighs, grabs the bright yellow ring that will punch him out of the aircraft, and pulls. A lot of things happen very quickly, seemingly all at once.

Inside the ejection seat a complicated series of carefully sequenced events play out automatically and almost instantaneously: the pilot's feet are pulled back against the seat by cables, his shoulders are retracted firmly against the seat back. Guillotine knives slice through electrical cables, separating the seat from the rest of the aircraft. Small explosive charges detonate, blowing the canopy away from the tumbling wreckage of the airframe. Finally, a rocket motor under the seat ignites; O'Grady and the seat are

(Above) The contents of the survival kit stored in the ejection seat include the radio, smoke and flare signals, flare gun and foliage-penetrating rockets, light sticks, matches, thermal blanket, survival rations, etc. The kit will normally dangle below you on a drop line, together with your life raft, once your parachute opens.

blasted clear of the dirty cloud of cartwheeling metal, into the deafening, sub-zero, 500-knot slipstream.

Although the ejection seat is designed to save your life, nobody guarantees you will enjoy the ride. Flail injuries are common in ejections - arms and legs broken by the fearsome wind blast. If a pilot is foolish enough to eject with his visor up he can expect eye and facial injuries; the visor and oxygen mask provide good protection as long as they stay in place, but nothing can protect the pilot from the wind and the amazing cold. On this occasion O'Grady lucks out: he suffers no serious injuries, although his neck is burned during the ejection.

A pilot strapped to an ejection seat makes a poor airfoil. Both tumble momentarily, then a drogue parachute deploys, stabilizing the seat. If the seat works properly it will be slowed to a safe and stable velocity. The pilot will continue to breathe oxygen from a small emergency bottle in the seat assembly. O'Grady, a reasonable guy, quickly tires of this modified free-fall through space while the ejection seat altitude sensors wait for a lower level before automatically deploying the main canopy. He elects to open the parachute manually; a tug on a handle on the side of the seat initiates the deployment sequence. The canopy assembly is popped from its container in the seat back, and begins to inflate while the bonds that lash the pilot to the seat itself are finally severed. At last the main canopy begins to deploy; the seat itself is finally cut loose from the pilot and falls away toward the ground, leaving O'Grady swinging in the harness.

Strapped to the parachute harness is a large survival kit, loaded with tools and supplies for just about any contingency and able to sustain a man for many days in extreme conditions. 2 June has been a day of extremes for Capt.O'Grady; while he has the bad luck to get hit by a missile, he has been fortunate to eject without damage to his personal fuselage or empenage. His flight leader doesn't know it, but O'Grady is alive and well - about 10,000 feet above the overrated attractions of rural Bosnia, with a good 'chute. While he sincerely congratulates himself on mere survival, it is not long before O'Grady also notices some Serbian soldiers - perhaps from the same unit that has just shot him down - gathering on the ground below him to watch his descent intently, and moving toward the spot where he will land.

O'Grady is lucky again: he lands without injury, by no means a foregone conclusion in these situations. Popping the quick-release fittings on the harness, he discards the parachute, dumps his helmet - and abandons the seat pack survival kit.... No matter how thorough the training, nothing can truly prepare a pilot for the disorienting effects of a real-life ejection at high speed and altitude, and in the tension of the moment he does not always act rationally.

With the enemy converging on him there is only one thing to do: run and hide. While he runs, O'Grady considers his resources: one 9mm pistol, a PRC-90 radio, a signal strobe, four tiny water bottles, a signal mirror, pencil flares, and not much more. His principal resource is the radio - and the training he received at the US Air Force's Survival, Evasion, Resistance, and Escape (SERE) school at Fairchild Air Force Base, Washington.

O'Grady keeps running, putting distance between himself and his pursuers. Finally, he finds a spot to hide and does his best to disappear into the undergrowth. He must have retained some of what he was taught on the SERE course, because when the Serbs show up to collect their politically invaluable prize they can't find him anywhere. They comb the scrub, sometimes walking within five feet of the pilot, but never see him. This game of hide and seek continues for days. The pilot rations his four little

(Below) The Mylar survival blanket can also be used as a water still; stretched over a hole in the ground with a container under its weighted center, it will collect condensation during the cool of the night.

(Above) The SRU-21/P survival vest worn by nearly all combat aircrew contains about seven to ten pounds of signalling and survival gear, including a radio and a pistol. This Marine Hornet pilot's vest includes a small bottle of drinking water, secured to the vest with "dummy cord".

packets of water, but they are finally exhausted. There's more in the seat pack survival kit, plus food and other necessities; but the Serbs have that now. O'Grady's one real hope is the PRC-90, a little radio about the size of a small book. Similar models have been around for thirty years and have saved the lives of hundreds of pilots in combat zones around the world. The "Prick-90" is a line-of-sight transceiver; if you can see a plane overhead you can probably talk to it, but the guy on the other side of the hill won't be able to hear you. It allows communication by Morse code or voice, and it also transmits a "beacon" signal on a "guard" frequency monitored by all US military aircraft. Although the radio doesn't draw much power, its little battery is only good for fourteen hours in beacon mode; O'Grady rations its use with extreme care.

Night falls. The pilot does what he was taught to do on the SERE course: move carefully away from danger, don't panic, keep up hope of rescue. He is cold, hungry, and afraid; later, he will say he was "like a scared little bunny rabbit, trying to hide." The Serbs continue the search into the night, firing their rifles and even rocket-propelled grenades into places where they think he may be hiding; the pilot continues to escape and evade, sleeping during the day, moving only between midnight and four in the morning. Two cows and a cowherd wander over to his hiding place, one of the cows grazing at his feet. O'Grady smears dirt on his face for camouflage, worms his way deeper into the brush, and keeps his head down. The cows amble off; O'Grady suppresses thoughts of hamburger, and waits. His chance comes on Day Four.

One of the NATO aircraft searching overhead picks up his beacon on the "guard channel", 243.0 MHz. The odd, "dipping" chirp of the PRC-90's beacon transmission is unmistakable - all military pilots know the sound and understand its significance. They don't know who is operating it, but they all know O'Grady is on the ground below - maybe dead, maybe a captive, maybe on the run. "Basher Five Two", he whispers into the PRC-90. The AWACS crew call the pilot on the guard channel to authenticate the transmission:

"Basher Five Two, this is Basher One One on Alpha", the AWACS controller calls at 0208 hours (local), from far away and high in the night sky. O'Grady tries to respond, but the little radio's range for voice

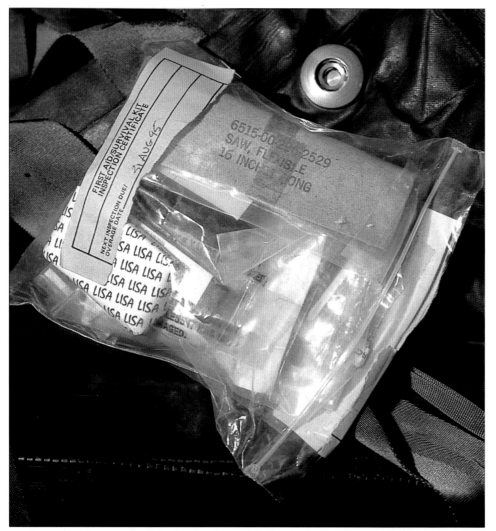

(**Left**) Some units fine-tune the contents of their survival kits with special extras; pilots of the 144th Fighter Wing get a flexible wire saw, a fishing kit, a small bar of soap, and other supplies in the seat pack.

(**Right**) The oxygen regulator block and the connection for the mike and earphones in the helmet attach directly to the survival vest. When you depart from the cockpit in the ejection seat you are thus far less likely to have the hose spring back and hit you in the face, as was once common.

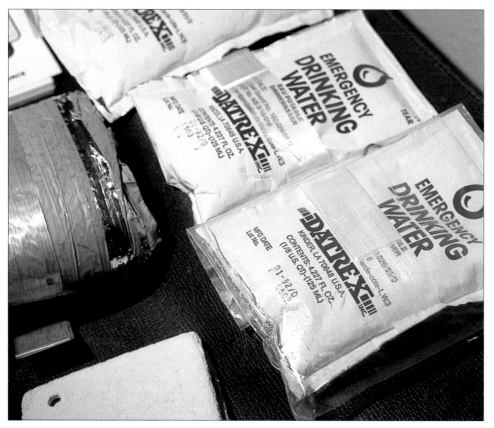

(**Left**) These little four-ounce packets of water sustained Captain O'Grady for several days. You can survive for literally weeks without solid food - O'Grady managed four days on bugs and berries without serious effects - but only a few days without water.

communication is fairly limited; the AWACS crew hears him transmit but can't copy the message. "Say again through Basher One One", O'Grady hears on the PRC-90. The pilot whispers into the little microphone, down in the Bosnian weeds; now the AWACS can hear him, but they aren't sure who they are talking to.

"Basher One One has you loud and clear! Who is this?" More static this time. "You're unreadable. I can barely hear you. Say call sign."

"Basher Five Two! Basher Five Two!", O'Grady replies, as loud as he dares.

"Okay", says AWACS, "understand you are Basher Five Two."

"I'm alive, I'm alive!" O'Grady says.

"Copy that!" But AWACS knows anybody with a little information from a captured pilot and a PRC-90 can lure a rescue force into disaster. The drill now is to authenticate the identity of the pilot.

"What was your squadron in Korea?" "Juvat, Juvat!" O'Grady responds. That's the right answer.

"Copy that! You are alive! It's good to hear your voice!"

A special US Marine Corps TRAP (tactical recovery of aircraft personnel) unit from the 24th Marine Expeditionary Unit (MEU) aboard the assault helicopter carrier USS Kearsarge has been waiting for the call. It comes almost immediately: "Execute."

The first helicopter lifts off at 0508, just at sunrise; then the rescue mission launches in two waves at 0550 hours aboard two big CH-53 helicopters, supported by a pair of AV-8B Harrier jump-jets and another pair of Cobra attack helicopters. The rescue flight forms up, orbits the carrier, then drops down to low altitude and blasts to the north. It takes ten minutes to cross the beach; "feet dry!" calls the lead pilot.

The flight hears O'Grady's beacon at 0612 hours and adjusts course to home on the chirping on 243.0. Only as the flight clears the last ridge does anybody actually talk to the pilot on the ground. Just as he was trained, O'Grady has selected a good landing zone (LZ) for the choppers; he describes it to the Cobras, then uses the Mk 13 combination flare/smoke signalling device to mark the spot. Dash One, the lead CH-53, eases into the LZ, aft cargo door open. Twenty heavily armed Marine infantrymen pour out of the aircraft and set up perimeter security for the extraction, ready to fire at the first sign of opposition from any hostile force. O'Grady materializes from the treeline, pistol in hand, and runs for the second helicopter, Dash Two. Within a few seconds he has been dragged through the door and strapped in a seat, wrapped in a blanket. "I'm ready to get the hell out of here!" O'Grady yells over the noise. "Get that pistol away from him!", Col. Marty Berndt, the mission commander, yells back. They both got their wish.

The ride back out to the Kearsarge is brief, but eventful. Two shoulder-launched SAMs are fired at the helicopters, but both miss. Serbian troops fire machine-guns at the choppers as they blast by overhead, at 175 knots and 150 feet off the deck, skimming the trees; they score hits in the fuselage, the tail rotor - and one bullet punctures a sergeant's canteen. But flight lead calls "feet wet" at 0715 hours as the package heads back across the beach. Fifteen minutes later O'Grady is aboard the carrier, safe and sound.

(Left) USAF Sergeant Troy Arce is in the Combat Search and Rescue business. The knee pads are necessary because he spends a lot of his time kneeling to peer over the door sill of a helicopter; the special armor vest and the pistol are necessary in case he encounters locals who don't want US aircrew rescued.

(Above & right) Sgt.Debbie Gifford and SSgt.Steven Robertson belong to Golf Company, 140th Aviation Regiment, a US Army National Guard CH-47 Chinook unit. Although "weekend warriors" once had the reputation for a kind of "country club" style and low-stress operations, this is no longer true. They frequently conduct "real world" rescues, and are often called in to help save lives during floods and forest fires. As well as being crew members on flight status, both these NCOs are unit Aviation Life Support Equipment (ALSE) technicians.

They wear here an innovative survival vest designed and manufactured for the specialized requirements of helicopter crews; the "gunner's belt" normally worn by the crew chief interfered with the conventional vest, so Golf Company ALSEs invented this more compatible model. This kind of initiative is typical of ALSE shops in all the services, but particularly so among the Army specialists who, unlike their Air Force counterparts, actually get to fly in the aircraft as well as maintaining the flight kit.

(Top) Some seat survival packs include items like these heavy mitts for protection against cold, if the unit operates in areas of high altitude terrain or extremes of climate.

(Left) The AN/URT-33 is an automatic beacon which activates when the pilot separates from the ejection seat, transmitting a signal advertising the position and plight of the guy at the other end of its little tether.

CHAPTER 2
All Dressed Up With Someplace To Go

Captain O'Grady could not have survived his mission on 2 June 1995 without the help of some very specialized and extremely interesting personal equipment and clothing. Military aviation is still as dangerous a business as it has been since the First World War; and in response to all the natural hazards and human malice faced by combat aircrew a wide range of helmets, flight suits, boots, underwear, anti-G clothing, gloves, and survival gear have been developed to protect them as far as possible. Virtually everything O'Grady wore or carried that day was designed to help him survive - and they all worked.

While the aircraft themselves generally get the attention and the glory, these items of aviator kit are sometimes just as important to the success of a combat mission as a fighter's turning radius or an attack helicopter's weapon systems. A properly fitted G-suit can prevent GLOC - the high gravity load-induced loss-of-consciousness which is as potentially lethal to a multi-million dollar aircraft as a heat-seeking AAM; and specialized helmets like the AH-64 Apache's IHADSS integrate the pilot into the airframe in ways that allow him to designate and engage targets merely by looking at them.

It has been quite a long time since I drew my first issue of flight gear from Supply at the 8th Transportation Helicopter Company at Qui Nhon, Republic of Vietnam; I was eighteen years old, and a brand new helicopter door gunner in what was then a new war. We each got a helmet, body armor, flight suits, leather flight gloves, a knife (which I still own), a PRC-6 rescue radio, and a little syrette of morphine. I got to know that gear well, and to appreciate its excellence; it was obvious that a lot of thought and testing had gone into every little detail. The helmets, armor, flight suits, gloves, and radios issued today are similar in design and intent, but even better thanks to superior materials like the Nomex fire-resistant fabrics used in the gloves and flight suits.

Although I am old enough to be the father of most of

(Above) Major Fredric "Lance" Olson, executive officer of the Marines' VMFA(AW)-225 "Vikings", an F/A-18 squadron, fastens his gear preparatory to baby-sitting the author for an hour-and-a-half aloft in a Hornet from El Toro air station in 1992. Note the BDU camouflage material made into a cover for the helmet, a not uncommon sight among ground attack crews and other aviators whose missions may take them low over scenery with hostile inhabitants.

today's combat fliers, I recently had a chance to go through the training and qualification process to fly in US Marine Corps fighters; it was a fascinating experience, and apart from other insights it underlined for me the differences in the physical challenge between my kind of flying thirty years ago and the working environment of today's "fast movers". Here's some of what you have to do before you can strap a high-performance military aircraft to your backside and go for a ride.

The Chamber Card and Swim Test
Nobody gets to strap on the helmet, "power pants", survival vest, and associated gear required for a ride in a "fast mover" without a lot of training - and some rather rigorous testing. There are similar training sessions and tests for helicopter crews, too. And you don't go through this gruelling process just once, but every three years or so, just to make sure you haven't become too feeble in body or mind in the interim.

There is good reason for this challenging program. Routine flight in military aircraft is fairly stressful; during an emergency this stress goes right off the scale. Every crash and major incident is investigated; and nearly all investigations reveal that pilots and crew members of combat aircraft, despite all their training, often do apparently stupid things when the normal routine is disrupted by an ejection or even by lower-level disasters.

The Air Force, Marine Corps, and Navy all conduct training to try to prepare fliers to deal with these emergencies, and all have roughly similar programs. I recently attended the USAF's Flight Physiology course at Edwards Air Force Base, California, as a prerequisite to flying with the US Marine Corps' VMFA-225, a F/A-18 Hornet outfit. You don't fly without a "chamber card", an orange certificate (unsuitable for framing) from one of the programs authorized to provide this training, plus another form (a NATOPS document for the US Navy and Marine Corps) attesting that your "quals" on survival gear are current. Both involve classwork, tests, and some rigorous physical evaluation.

(Left) Captain Dave Bonner, an AV-8B Harrier II pilot of the Marines' VMA-231 "Aces", checks the fit of his oxygen mask before a flight from MCAS Cherry Point in 1991. Capt.Bonner flew around 40 missions during the Gulf War, but did not have to practice his escape-and-evasion skills.

(Below) The visible lower part of the model of life preserver issued to US Navy and Marine fliers. A solid tug on the beads - more easily locatable by touch alone than the rings or tapes used on a previous generation of "Mae Wests" - will inflate the device. This is to be avoided while still in the cockpit..

(Left) The US Air Force life preserver, the LPU-9/P, with its slightly more visible "horse collar" bladder stowage.

(Above) To a pilot's eyes, an ugly sight even during a training session in a calm, sunlit pool: Major Ryan Orian demonstrates what happens during one of the flier's special, claustrophobic nightmares - when the deployed parachute canopy comes down on top of you after a jump into the open ocean. In "real world" emergencies this can kill you; aircrew need training to avoid panic and find their way safely out from under.

Classes deal with the effects of hypoxia or oxygen deprivation - a sneaky, scary condition that happens when the pressurization system in your aircraft quits working. These failures sometimes creep up on you gradually, and sometimes grab you with dramatic suddenness. The instructors at Edwards AFB tell the story of the F-14 Tomcat crew cruising along over the Pacific who decided to unstrap from their ejection seats – and "moon" their wingmen! Their flight mates alongside observed this performance in astonishment, which turned to real alarm as they watched the jet drop away. Frantic radio transmissions failed to rouse the crew from their irrational state; and the aircraft crashed with the loss of both men. That's the kind of thing that people do when they aren't getting enough oxygen. The warning signs are subtle, progressive, and quite individual, and aircrew are trained to watch out for them in themselves and in others. That training begins with a day and a half of lectures, followed by the infamous "chamber ride".

The chamber is a large steel tank with seating for about ten people. Once everybody is inside, with oxygen masks fitted and operating, the hatch is secured and a large compressor starts pumping the air out of the chamber. The effect replicates a ride in an unpressurized aircraft to over 30,000 feet, but without the cold temperatures; some bloating and a few rude noises are quite normal, but the instructors watch carefully for people who may not be using the mask correctly, or who begin to panic, or otherwise develop physiological problems.

Once "up at altitude" you are instructed to unmask, and thereafter to pay special attention to the color of your fingertips, your ability to converse, and your

(Left) Major Danny Cerna of the 144th Fighter Wing training with the LPU-9T. All variants of the life preserver are designed to do the same basic job - not just to keep you afloat, but also to keep your face out of the water, even if you are unconscious and your head is still weighted down by your helmet.

(Below) Safely escaped from the clammy and potentially lethal embrace of his canopy, Major Orian prepares to clamber aboard the little one-man life raft. The trick is to start at the small end, submerge it, and slide it beneath you. The raft will be full of water - but it will be full of you, too, and the water can be bailed out later. In a calm swimming pool it's not a hard knack to master; in freezing darkness, with choppy waves slapping you around, it can be a different story.

(Right) A whole military profession keeps the "brain buckets" and "speed jeans" neat, clean and well-maintained: the Aviation Life Support Equipment specialists, like this Marine ALSE technician serving with VMFA-225 "Vikings" at El Toro. Few ever get to fly with the gear which they look after, but even so they are a dedicated band.

reasoning ability. You are instructed to do simple mathematics problems, and to respond to orders from the instructor. Everybody is expected to experience hypoxia to some verifiable degree. I noticed my fingertips turn blue, and I started to have trouble getting simple words down on paper. One guy on the same ride became loud and somewhat argumentative, and a woman started to giggle uncontrollably. The effect was somewhat like having too much to drink, but without warning signs. After a while our aggressively hypoxic companion was ordered to remask; he could not do it - would not do it. He babbled on while the instructors yelled at him, over and over again, to put on his mask; finally, one of the instructors had to do it for him. His recovery was quite rapid, but afterwards he didn't remember any of his odd behaviour. It was quite an object lesson in the hazards of hypoxia.

Finally, before they let you out of the chamber, you get a demonstration of the effects of explosive decompression - the rapid loss of cabin pressurization that happens when the skin of the aircraft is punctured at altitude. This is demonstrated with the students seated in a smaller, sealed portion of the chamber, with oxygen masks off and regulators in the "off" position. When one of the instructors pops the valve, most of the air is sucked right out of the chamber with a bang. A cloud of vapour makes visibility difficult. You are quite suddenly at about 30,000 feet, and if you fail to mask up properly and turn your regulator

on correctly you will begin to feel the effects of hypoxia in a very short time.

It takes more than the chamber card to fly with the Marines, and one of the other required qualifications is the "swim test". No special training is given before the test; you just show up at the pool at the appointed time, then suit up in full kit - flight suit, boots, survival vest, helmet, speed jeans. Then you jump in for a ten minute drown-proofing session, followed by a couple of laps of the pool, still in your full kit. It sounds worse than it actually is, although if you have your vest adjusted too snugly breathing becomes extremely difficult. But the "speed jeans" hold a little air, and that provides a degree of buoyancy. The hard part is maintaining good form for the instructor while wearing all that stuff.

If you survive a trip to the far end of the pool and back there is only one final challenge to overcome: the life raft. You must manoeuver yourself aboard a little one-man raft - again, not too difficult even with the helmet and boots. Essentially, all you have to do is submerge one end of the raft and slide it beneath you from the back, then slither backwards aboard. Once you've proved you can wrestle successfully with a bobbing dinghy, congratulations - you're "good to go".

In the Ready Room
The "bone domes", "speed jeans" and other assorted equipment is so complex and important that every aviation unit includes several personnel whose full-time job it is to care for flight gear. These Aviation Life

Support Equipment (ALSE) specialists can spend an entire career managing and maintaining the equipment - and never once get a ride in the aircraft (that is especially true with fighter units, less so with helicopter outfits). You will find them constantly cleaning oxygen masks, testing regulators, inspecting survival gear, and mending all kinds of kit. They will issue your equipment and make sure it is properly fitted. Be nice to them - your survival may be in their hands.

How and where you dress for a flight will depend a lot on what you're flying. Helicopter crews tend to amble out to the aircraft in just their flight suits, carrying helmet bags and survival gear, and putting these on once they get out to the flight line. Fighter crews suit up at the ready room lockers, and wear everything except the helmet out to the aircraft. Regardless, the foundations tend to be identical for both. If you get invited for a ride in a US combat aircraft, cotton or Nomex underwear and socks are mandatory, not an

option: the synthetics found in many fabrics today will melt when exposed to fire, sticking to your body and causing aggravated burn injuries - cotton will not.

Over their underwear most US military fliers then pull on the one-piece coverall flight suit designated CWU-27/P (or -28). The flight suit comes in two colors, sage green or orange, but nearly all fashionable fliers go for the sage green version, particularly for flights over enemy territory. Sizes from 36S to 48R will accommodate anybody from midget to monster.

The suit zips up the front, and Velcro tapes adjust the waist. There are pockets just about everywhere: two breast pockets, one on the sleeve designed for pens and pencils (and as handy for cigarettes), pockets on the thighs and on the lower legs. There is even a curious little pocket on the inside of the left thigh, complete with lanyard, designed to accommodate the MC-1 pocket knife. This knife is supposed to be stowed with the lanyard wrapped around and hooked blade extended for emergency use, particularly for cutting parachute shroud lines. (I have never yet seen this pocket used for its designed function, however; and actually having a knife in the knife pocket will cost you a round of drinks in the squadron bar at some units.) In one of the breast pockets many pilots will stow a couple of brown paper "barf bags" - even fighter pilots and weapons officers get airsick, and if you are ever going to get nauseous it will certainly be during air combat manoeuvers.

This coverall is made of Nomex, a remarkable fabric that has prevented many of the severe burn injuries that were once all too common among military

(Left) Ready room, VMFA-225, MCAS El Toro, California: this F/A-18D Hornet pilot or "wizzo" (Weapons System Officer) is one of the many aircrew who like to decorate their helmet bags with the patches of all their previous units.

(Below) US Air Force MSgtJoseph De Simas III presides over the 144th Fighter Wing's parachute loft, where he is seen repacking a 'chute from the F-16's ACES II ejection seat.

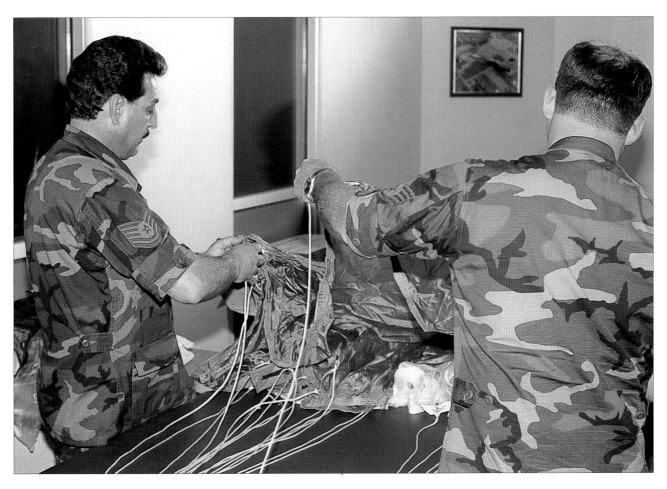

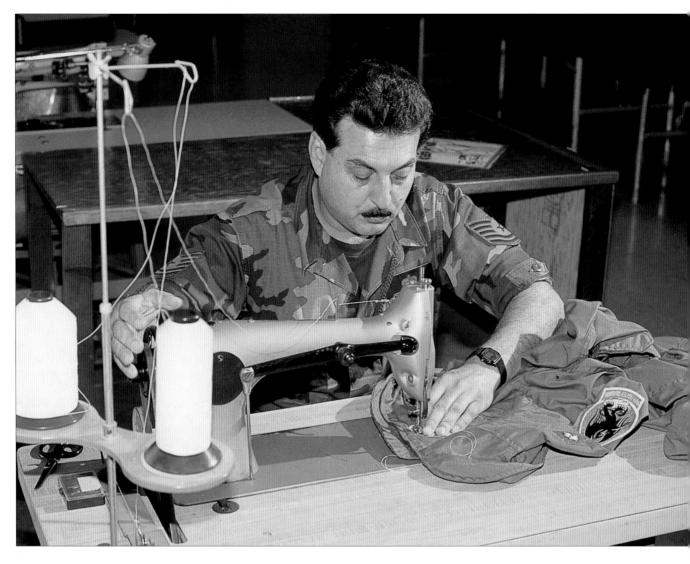

(Above) Virtually all ALSE specialists are skilled tailors. The garments they match up to their customers' requirements are more expensive than a Savile Row suit, fit better, and are worn to some of the most interesting and exclusive "affairs" in the world.... MSgt.De Simas working on a flight suit for one of the 144th's fighter jocks.

aircrew. It is a statistical fact of life that some aircraft will catch fire every month, and some crew members will be exposed to burning fuel. Nomex won't melt or burn under these conditions; it will char if it gets hot enough (about 700 degrees Fahrenheit), but it won't stick to the skin. Nomex has multiple virtues and is used extensively for aviator clothing and other military applications. It is light in weight, resists abrasion, and has the non-absorbent qualities of nylon. You can chuck the Nomex flight suit in the washing machine or send it to the cleaners - but hold the starch. Despite movies like *"Top Gun,"* the flight suit wasn't designed to make you look cool, but to keep you cool in a fire. The sleeves have even been intentionally designed so most people can't even roll them up; this keeps your arms covered - important when the aircraft catches fire.

You will also be issued a pair of GS/FRP-2 flight gloves; these get stowed in one of the pockets until you're in the aircraft, but they are an important additional protection against fire. The palms are made of a thin, soft cabretta leather. Properly fitted, these gloves are extremely comfortable, and they are popular with people throughout the armed forces; you'll often see them worn by Army Green Berets, Navy SEALs, Recon Marines, and anybody else who knows where to pilfer them or is willing to shell out $35 for a pair.

Heavy boots are required, even though the walk to the flight line is short. If you eject or crash land boots will protect your feet during the event; and if you have to walk out from the crash site your boots will quickly mean the difference between mobility and injury in the kind of remote, broken terrain falling aircraft seem to prefer as impact points. Naturally, pilots are not always content with the standard issue, tried and true, leather boots. While you can buy your own pair, the Army (in AR 95-1) and most other services require that they be leather.

As an example of why the armed forces require the traditional material, consider the case of one senior Army pilot whose nylon boots were exposed to fire during a crash; the nylon began to melt and shrink, tightening around the feet and transferring heat to the skin. A severe injury resulted, and the pilot was taken off flight status for a long recuperation. A leather boot would have prevented the injury entirely; another Army pilot, wearing a pair of the "Matterhorn" mountain boots popular with Rangers, actually ran through a pool of burning JP-4 fuel to escape from a crash. Although the nylon laces and some of the stitching melted, along with a portion of the sole of the boot, the pilot's foot was well insulated and his feet were uninjured.

If you're scheduled for a hop in a "fast mover", now is the time to put on your "speed jeans" or "power pants" - the anti-G suit. This is an inflatable bladder cut much like a cowboy's chaps. The ALSE specialists will have checked and fitted your pair; they zip up the side, with the inlet hose dangling from the left side. The survival vest comes next; then you strap on the harness that will clip on to the parachute stowed in the ejection seat. Your helmet and oxygen mask go in the helmet bag, along with your knee board, charts, notebook, and a spare "barf bag".

And now that you cut a suitably dashing and intrepid figure, it is time to waddle awkwardly down the hall to one of the briefing rooms where our fearless leader will give us the bad news about today's excursion...

(Above left & right) Aircrew the world over cannot resist decorating their coveralls and jackets with patches - the gaudier the better. The invention of Velcro, that invaluable material, has saved an awful lot of sewing, apart from making comfortable size adjustment of flight suits a great deal quicker and easier. Here Capt.Roland Aguilar, in 1992 an F-111 Aardvark pilot with the 524th Tactical Fighter Training Squadron, 27th Tactical Fighter Wing at Cannon AFB, New Mexico, models the CWU-27 flight suit from the right, and Lt. Craig Hunnicutt from the left. Conventionally, rank is worn on the shoulders, the squadron patch on the right sleeve, the patch of the wing or other higher formation on the left sleeve, that of the command on the right chest, and the wings/name patch on the left chest.

(Left) February 1992: an F-111 Ardvark crew of the 522nd TFS, 27th TFW suit up by their individual lockers at Cannon AFB, New Mexico. It can be cold in the desert at this time of year, and they wear over their coveralls the CWU-45/P winter flight jacket. Made of fireproof Nomex like the suit, it can withstand temperatures up to 350 degrees Centigrade.

(Below) Combat Edge helmets and flight gear hanging ready at the 144th Fighter Wing. While some units provide individual lockers for the gear, many others use shelves and hooks in a common area so that ALSE techs can have access at all times for routine maintenance.

(Previous page, above & opposite
Immediately after receiving their brief for a practice mission, "Vikings" of VMFA-225 gird their loins in the ready room. Marine and Navy pilots have this big snap-link attached to the right shoulder of their parachute harness to make rescue hoisting to a helicopter reasonably quick and safe; Air Force pilots need a "horse collar" or alternative system fitted on the hoist cable to winch them out of harm's way.

(Right) Major Danny Cerna, an F-16 pilot of the 144th Fighter Wing, removes his "power pants" after a flight, undoing the third zipper. The anti-gravity pants are carefully fitted to each pilot by the squadron ALSE technicians; thereafter, as long as the pilot hasn't been hitting the pasta too hard, getting into them is fairly quick and easy. First you wrap the upper portion around your midsection, attaching it with two hooks and then fastening this zipper on the right side; the left leg is then positioned and zipped up, followed by the right leg.

(Left) The importance of a good, solid pair of leather boots will instantly become clear to any aircrew whose ship catches fire. Serious footwear is modelled here by USAF C-21 pilots Lieutenants Greg Short and Jolin Barriere at Naval Air Station Fallon, Texas. (Photo Robert Genat)

(Below) The standard issue GS/FRP-2 flight gloves made from Nomex and cabretta leather are an extremely popular design; comfortable, flexible, and providing good protection against fire, they will also be seen in use by various Special Forces personnel, and many other service people who can "organise" themselves a pair "through channels", or are willing to shell out $35. They are worn here by the Army pilot of a 3rd Helicopter Brigade (Attack) AH-64 Apache at Fort Hood, Texas.

(Left) USAF F-15E Strike Eagle crewman of the 336th TFS, 4th TFW carrying helmet bags out to the flight line with, typically, his parachute harness left unfastened until the last moment. Then the straps hanging on his butt will be unfastened and pulled forward between the legs, passing outwards over the hips to re-engage these D-rings and snap-hooks. To function safely in an emergency the harness has to grip so tightly that comfortable walking is impossible once it has been fastened.

(Far left) A Tomcat crew from VF-202 head out to the flight line under the Texan sun at US Naval Air Station Fallon, 1990. Note the Navy fliers' HGU-33 helmet, the life preserver details, and the leg restraint straps. (Photo Robert Genat)

(Left & below) Two angles on the pilot and WSO of a USAF F-4G Phantom II "Wild Weasel" of the 561st TFS photographed in 1991. Note the slightly different set-up of the survival vest as compared with the Navy crew opposite.

Another F-14 Tomcat crew from Navy Reserve squadron VF-202 (their suit sleeves adorned with their squadron patch and the flag of the state of Texas) climb in and strap in, with help from their crew chief. Again, note details of USN helmets and life preserver, ejection seat, and parachute harness attached to risers of the 'chute stowed in the seat. (Photos Robert Genat)

(**Left**) An EA-6B crewman from USN Reserve Air Wing 30 at NAS Fallon, 1991, strides purposefully out to exercise his calling. Just what is it about this guy's outline that brings to mind the phrase "I *am* the law..."? (Photo Robert Genat)

CHAPTER 3

Power Pants and Brain Buckets: Fashionable Attire Aloft

(Left) Lieutenants Ray Toth and Dan Holmes, a US Air Force F-15E crew from the 336th Fighter Squadron ("Rocketeers") at Seymour Johnson AFB in 1991, model the flight suit, anti-G pants, Nomex gloves, regulation boots, survival vest (note slight differences in pocket placement even between this WSO and his pilot), and HGU-55 helmet; life preservers are not worn here.

(Above & overleaf) Pure nostalgic self-indulgence for the author: a couple of shots from inside a T-28 Trojan - the type in which, during a gun-and-rocket run over Vietnam, he first felt multiple gravities squishing his internal organs down into his boots. The helmets here are HGU-33s. (Photos Robert Genat)

Just about everything issued by the ALSE specialists has been developed and manufactured by the Gentex Corporation, headquartered in Carbondale, Pennsylvania, in close co-operation with the USAF's Armstrong Laboratory at Brooks Air Force Base in Texas. Gentex has been designing and making helmets for aviators almost since Wilbur and Orville slipped the surly bonds of earth back at the beginning of the century. They currently make every helmet in this book, plus the oxygen mask, speed jeans, and new Combat Edge "speed tuxedo" used in the F-15 and F-16. Gentex actually developed a lot of these designs, under contract to the Department of Defense. They make the fabric, bond the laminates and mold the masks, pretty much "in-house". This interesting outfit is unknown to most people outside the military; but when it comes to aviator kit, Gentex is a combined Lockheed/ McDonnell-Douglas/ Boeing/ Bell-Textron kind of place, where new systems are imagined, designed, perfected, and put into service.

Until you've actually strapped an F-16 or F/A-18 to your rear end and gone aloft over the tactical training ranges north of Nellis AFB in Nevada, or out over the Pacific near El Toro Marine Air Station, you really can't appreciate the value and virtue of all the kit Gentex makes and the US Government issues. In fact, if your idea of flying a fighter comes from movies like "Top Gun" or similar fantasies, you may have a shock coming. In the movies fighter pilots wear really cool sunglasses and let their oxygen masks dangle unclipped, so we can see their wry grins and shiny teeth. Tom Cruise gets a kind of mild ride through space; it looks like fun. Well, as neophyte fighter pilot candidates learn on their first flight at the Air Force Academy, it isn't always fun - and for some people the experience is pure hell. Modern fighters are designed to be agile, to twist and turn, hard. Even ground attack aircraft load up on the Gs during pull-outs from cannon and rocket runs. The human body is designed to operate at optimum levels of comfort and efficiency at one dull, basic, earthbound G; when first exposed to multiple gravities it reacts in ways its tenant will find quite memorable.

Any real fighter jocks in the audience will probably think the following anecdote about my own first fighter ride is pretty funny; the G-loads were light, and the "fighter" was a little T-28 prop-trainer. On the other hand, unlike today's pros, my first fighter hop was on a combat mission in a combat zone. Virtually every fighter pilot learns the business in a careful, progressive way. There are months of screening, testing and classroom studies; then a lot of hours in a

(Previous page) "Speed jeans aren't really designed to make you fly better ", claims one aircrew; "they make your tummy look small and your manly bits look especially manly". Nevertheless, even the crews of prop-driven US Marine Corps observation aircraft - like these OV-10 Bronco riders from VMO-2 - wear them to help control the oxygen supply to the brain during sharp low-altitude turns and pull-outs. Note typical USMC/USN life preserver, survival vest and 'chute harness set-up. (Photo Robert Genat)

(Left) "Jeez, you aren't really going to make us do that dumb 'thumbs up' thing, are you?" Well, yes, actually we are. Brightly decorated helmets, like the HGU-33/Ps worn by these two Navy aviators, used to be high fashion; many even featured added reflective tape. In due course somebody decided that while they might be spiffy, they could also be seen - and perhaps shot at - from a long way off. Puritan gray is nowadays the norm. (Photo Robert Genat)

(Opposite top left) Rear detail of USAF parachute harness assembly, showing personal lowering device.

(Opposite top right) USAF F-16 pilot Captain Tandy Bozeman, 144th FW, wears part of the new Combat Edge assembly now issued to F-15 and F-16 pilots, complete with life preserver

primary trainer and intermediate trainers; then finally the real thing - check-out and more training in F-15s or F/A-18s. After a great deal more training our hero will possibly get shipped off to a combat zone, years after entering the pipeline. But not everybody comes to this experience as the peak of such a leisurely escalation.

As mentioned earlier, I spent part of my dissolute youth as a helicopter door gunner in Vietnam. Since not all crews participated in every operation, we were sometimes left on the ground while most of the 8th Trans conducted an assault. On one of these occasions I hitched a ride with a Vietnamese Air Force pilot flying combat support for the assault. The T-28s shared our field, and normally flew with the back seat empty. A request to one of the pilots was granted - as long as I brought along my own parachute. A seat pack 'chute was "borrowed" from another unit on the field; and off we went, right after the helicopters launched, just after dawn. The VNAF captain made the take-off, sucked the wheels up, trimmed the T-28 for climb out, and called, "You've got it." I climbed up, into the cool air over the Central Highlands toward the little village and dirt strip at a place called Ahn Khe where the helicopters loaded the infantry. We orbited overhead while they took off again, formed up, and headed for the landing zones. Since I had very little time in any kind of aircraft my formation flying abilities were somewhat limited, but I did manage to keep

within a thousand feet or so of the assigned altitude - with the wingman keeping a noticeably respectful distance.

When the helos were about ten minutes out from the LZ the VNAF captain took the controls back, pushed the throttle full forward, and got busy arming the .50 cal. machine guns and rocket pods attached to the pylons. With the choppers just a couple of minutes out and clearly in sight, we pushed over from about 10,000 feet. The old T-28 was never supposed to be more than a trainer for more capable aircraft, but - as it has proved in many different national liveries - it was just about perfect for this kind of ground-attack mission. We roared down out of the sky at full power, nearly vertical. Big fireballs appeared in front of the wing as the machine guns laid down suppressive fire on targets around the LZ. Then the captain hauled back on the stick.

It was only a four-or five-G manoeuver, but I felt invisible forces dragging me down toward the floor of the cockpit - it was a sickening sensation. Soon we were back at altitude again, but the captain was not through yet. He pushed over and we repeated the whole performance, this time launching the rockets in a long, rippling, fiery salvo.

If you think the pull-out at the bottom of a gun run (even in a T-28) is fun and games for an inexperienced pilot, you're mistaken. During the lengthy training which is conventional for people in

this line of work you learn to anticipate and manage the effect of the Gs; and those were lessons I hadn't been taught. My head was forced down by a giant, invisible hand until all I could see was the floor. I could feel my blood draining toward my boots. I really couldn't understand how the guy up front was functioning with such apparently matter-of-fact ease while I was having such difficulty just trying to figure out where my internal organs were heading. It was extremely uncomfortable and disorienting, and my greatest satisfaction from the flight was that I didn't actually throw up.

The G-forces that are an inherent part of air combat manoeuvering (even in a T-28) are a physical stress on the human body that needs to be managed and controlled. You can develop a tolerance for them, but only by enduring them over and over again. You can learn how to brace yourself in the seat, how to breathe, how to tense the abdominal muscles, grunt, and still function. Anybody who wants to fly close-quarter combat in a fighter needs to be able to tolerate up to nine positive Gs - a load that will render most people quite unconscious in just a few seconds. Indeed, many experienced pilots claim that positive G forces can become almost fun (though nobody I know likes negative G forces, the kind that force blood into your head rather than away from it).

Combat pilots were trained to counter these effects even before World War II. To raise positive G tolerance their instructors told them to tense the muscles of the abdomen, arms and legs; to strain against the seat belt and harness; and to push against the rudder pedals. It was well known, then as now, that short, stocky pilots generally tolerated G-loads better than tall, skinny ones; and that lack of sleep, lack of oxygen, and overindulgence in booze or tobacco all increased the negative effects of G-loads on a pilot.

"Speed jeans", and the new Combat Edge "speed tuxedo", help prevent the flow of blood from the head during air combat manoeuvers at over four Gs. This keeps the pilot's brain functional while trying to acquire or evade a lock-on. A good fighter pilot can keep his head up and "check six" even at nine G; beginners have a hard time functioning at half that level. The simple fact is that aircraft design has progressed enormously, and the puking pink body in the cockpit has not. The structure of modern fighters will tolerate a great deal more gravity than a human body can; Mikoyan claims that the MiG-29 will handle a lot more than eleven sustained Gs without problems, and American and British designs can probably perform just as well. Few, if any pilots can function for long at these loads, however. The pilots of American F-15 and F-16 fighters now have a new flight ensemble, designed and developed by Gentex, that allows them to pull more Gs and pull them longer than before.

"Speed jeans", "power pants" or "fast slacks" have been around in one version or another for fifty years, since World War II. This garment is a fairly simple item containing five inflatable bladders (one for each calf and thigh, plus one around the midsection), linked to a control unit in the aircraft. During high-G manoeuvers the control unit sends pressurized air to the bladders, inflating them; the result is a kind of half-body hug for the pilot, constricting major blood vessels and restricting the tendency of the pilot's blood to pool in the lower extremities. That keeps some blood, and therefore oxygen, available to the pilot's skull, where it is needed to keep his brain functional. Versions of this system have been used by generations of combat pilots in Korea, Vietnam, and numerous lesser encounters, and have performed well enough. But the trend in air combat tactics has been toward extremes of agility and away from pure speed; agility in air combat manoeuvering means extremely rapid and violent onset of G-loads, and new systems are always under development to provide the pilot with improved tolerance of the effects.

CSU-17/P Combat Edge

The latest ensemble, called "Combat Edge" by Gentex and the Air Force, uses a combination of "speed jeans", a kind of "speed vest", and a pressure breathing system which postpones the onset of GLOC. The system includes five major components: the helmet, oxygen mask, pressure vest, oxygen terminal block, and "speed jeans". While the latter are the same standard issue CSU-13 anti-G suit worn by other fighter and attack aircrew, the other four components are the latest state-of-the-art designs, each designed to help a pilot or weapons officer function during manoeuvers up to nine positive Gs.

Combat Edge Helmet - HGU-55

The HGU-55 resembles conventional US Air Force helmets, but close inspection reveals several differences. The basic shell is the same lightweight, close-fitting design as the earlier HGU-33, but the front opening is slightly wider for improved peripheral vision. Unlike the HGU-33, the Combat Edge model incorporates a black rubber tube running from the oxygen mask to the rear of the helmet; this tube provides automatic tensioning of the mask during the high-onset manoeuvers that would previously pull a mask away from the pilot's face, breaking the mask seal and reducing the supply of oxygen. One of the great virtues of the HGU-55 is its centre of gravity, closely matching that of the head inside it. This is more important than you might think, even though the helmet only weighs a pound and a half. The light weight is another virtue - a surprising one considering that the whole package includes noise-attenuating earphones, a visor assembly (clear for night missions, dark neutral gray for day use), the liner, plus the bayonet-receivers for the mask.

Each helmet is custom-fitted to the individual pilot,

(Opposite) Detail, attachment and adjustment point on harness for upper part of "horse collar" life preserver.

(Below) Detail, parachute harness: chest strap buckle assembly.

(Above) Even in the cockpit of a "fast mover" the modern warrior cannot escape paperwork; elastic straps are provided for it on the anti-gravity pants.

(Left) Detail, parachute harness: right attachment point for the ejection seat parachute riser.

who will keep it as permanent issue for as long as he (or, now, she) is on flight status. The ALSE technicians fit the new helmet to the pilot by removing the thermoplastic liner and heating it in an oven, then replacing it in the helmet; the pilot jams his head in this assembly, buckles the mask and chin strap on, and waits for the liner to cool. When it does it will retain a perfect fit to the individual skull, assuming that the nape strap and chin strap are adjusted properly. The shell itself is made of Kevlar, that revolutionary material with a thousand uses throughout the military and other strenuous pastimes. It comes in three sizes - Medium, Large, and Extra Large - to fit just about anybody the USAF will allow near an airplane. Gentex makes these, along with much of the product line, in their big factory at Carbondale, Pennsylvania.

Combat Edge Oxygen Mask - MBU-20/P
Proper fit and functioning of the mask is another

essential for combat aircrew, improved by the Combat Edge design designated MBU-20. The mask provides pressurized breathing oxygen to the pilot automatically through a system that kicks in at a predetermined G load - normally +4G. The mask incorporates the standard M-169A/AIC microphone for voice communication, and separate inlet and exhaust valves for lower respiration resistance. Silicone rubber is used for fabrication of most of the mask, although a composite hard-shell has been added to the traditional design to support the breathing hose, valves, and mike assembly.

You don the mask after the helmet is on and adjusted: the three-pin connector at the lower end of the breathing hose attaches to the regulator terminal block on the vest, the communications cord and plug assembly are fitted to the mating connectors on the aircraft, then the little black rubber PBG hose quick-disconnect attaches at the back of the helmet. The mask bayonet catches slide into the fittings on each side of the helmet. You can't breathe until you turn on the oxygen control panel in the cockpit. Wearing an oxygen mask for a long time can be rather uncomfortable, even with the best designs. There is a little resistance to each breath, even at 1G. They get hot and clammy, and the rubber sticks to your face after a while. Many pilots unmask below 10,000 feet, where the use of supplemental oxygen is not required, but this is not always such a good idea. The mask provides protection during an ejection; if it isn't being worn, it won't help when the wing falls off unexpectedly and you have a few microseconds to punch out of the cockpit.

Helmets For Every Occasion

The very first Mk 1 "brain bucket" must have been issued to a spearman somewhere in the Middle East about four thousand years ago. The basic idea was the same then as now - to prevent impact fractures of the brittle bone box enclosing the soft stuff that does the thinking; and the construction and design were not really that different from today, although the materials were. (Different does not mean worse, however: leather - a common material in helmet construction over the whole period since the dawn of recorded history - is still one of the best materials for impact protection, and actually rivals Kevlar under some specific circumstances. You won't find leather used in military helmets today, but it is interesting to note that it is making a comeback in head protection for firefighters in the USA.)

(Right) This US Marine CH-46 Sea Knight crew chief wears an SPH-4 helmet, and the bulky survival vest common among USMC helo crews. Although on this occasion in 1991 the helicopter was operating over the arid ranges of Twentynine Palms in California's Mojave Desert, the sergeant - whose outfit, HMM-166, was normally attached to the USS *Okinawa* (LPH-3) - still routinely carries a HEED bottle of emergency air in the big front left pocket.

(**Left, above & right**) Captain Bob "Tinker" Bell, an F/A-18 Hornet pilot with VMFA-225, poses in full USMC flight ensemble in tasteful shades of green, green, gray, green and green....Note the parachute harness leg straps fastened ready to emplane; the HGU-55/P helmet; the oxygen mask with regulator attached directly to the survival vest; and the belly fastening of the life preserver.

According to the the Army's Aeromedical Research Laboratory Biodynamics Research Division, the human head can tolerate an impact of about 30G on the nose, and a force of between 100 and 200G per square inch on the frontal bone of the skull, before something important (rather than merely cosmetic) breaks - and even more, if the impact is spread over a larger area. The helmet is designed to spread that impact out, and it works when the "brain bucket" is properly sized and fitted, with all the straps adjusted and secured.

About one crew member in five will lose his or her helmet in a crash. This normally occurs (two times out of three) when the chinstrap fails; other losses occur due to poorly adjusted suspensions or badly sized pads. The idea is for the chin strap and nape strap to form a tight ring at the base of the skull - the tighter the ring, the more likely the helmet is to stay put where it belongs.

There are many variants of two basic designs, one for helicopter flight and the other for crews in fast jets. While the designs for fighter crews are radically different from those of the past, the basic helicopter model is nearly identical to the helmet of thirty years ago and more.

SPH-4

The SPH-4 is a design that has been around practically since the Crusades. The current B model is almost identical to the version lots of us helicopter crew wore in Vietnam with many small, incremental improvements. The visor housing now accommodates a bracket for night vision goggles, and the shell is now made from Kevlar, with a thermoplastic liner instead of the foam rubber pads of the old version. The helmet hasn't changed much because its mission hasn't changed over the years. A helicopter aircrew helmet still has to provide protection for the skull against impact, for the eyes against debris and fragmentation spall, and for the ears against the tremendous noise inside any helicopter. The helmet provides support for communications through the boom microphone and the earphones, plus their associated wiring. New versions of the helicopter aircrew helmet (like the HGU-56/P) add a little extra protection against impact and noise, plus visors that fend off laser radiation - the new battlefield threat of directed energy weapons, already in use by some threat nations.

The SPH-4 is issued in two sizes, Regular and Extra Large. With all the communications gear and dual visors installed it weighs about three and a half pounds. That might not seem like much, but after a long day flying combat support missions in a Chinook your neck will begin to feel as if it's supporting a ton, and the earcups will leave odd-looking imprints on the side of your head. A small amount of discomfort is a low price to pay, however, for the helmet's superb protection from a very hostile environment.

SPH-5CG

Gentex developed a version of the basic military helicopter helmet for the US Coast Guard, the SPH-55CG. More than any other service, the little USCG has a real-world mission that keeps its crews hopping - often far off shore on dark and stormy nights. The Coast Guard version is metallic blue in color, fabricated from Graphlon composite, and features a bracket for the ANVIS-6 night vision goggle used by USCG aircrew.

IHADSS

The Army's Apache helicopter pilots are each issued a $10,000 helmet with a built-in television screen - a piece of kit which proves that today looks *can* kill, and which for old science fiction buffs recalls Robert Heinlein's classic *Starship Troopers*. This model is called IHADSS - the Integrated Helmet and Display Sight Subsystem. This large, exotic helmet allows the pilot to enjoy some of the same "head up" advantages as jet fighter pilots - the ability to receive weapons and navigation information without having to look down at his instruments. While the "fast mover" drivers get their data from a Head Up Display (HUD) of green figures and symbols created between the pilot's face and the windshield, the Apache pilot's similar display is projected on a small disk in front of his right eye; the visual display of selectable data is superimposed over anything the pilot looks at. Sensors on the bulkhead behind the helmet determine helmet and head orientation, and allow the pilot to "slave" the helicopter's cannon to the helmet: the pilot can aim the gun just by turning toward the target.

(**Right**) Marine AV-8B Harrier "jump jet" pilot Captain Dave Bonner wears essentially identical flight gear to Captain Bell. The helmets' white shells are nowadays normally "subdued" with a fabric cover or drab tape; but it is still typical that a squadron badge is displayed on the protective cover of the HGU-55's externally mounted visor. Apart from their oxygen mask control system, in Navy and Marine Corps service the HGU-55's communications wiring differs slightly from the USAF format.

(Left) The US Coast Guard is America's smallest, least appreciated armed force - with a set of big, challenging missions that demand high performance from aircraft and crews. This HH-65A helicopter pilot ready to launch from the USCG's San Francisco air station wears the special SPH-5CG helmet developed for the Coast Guard, with the insulated flight suit worn by crews flying over the frigid North Pacific, and a combination life preserver/survival vest.

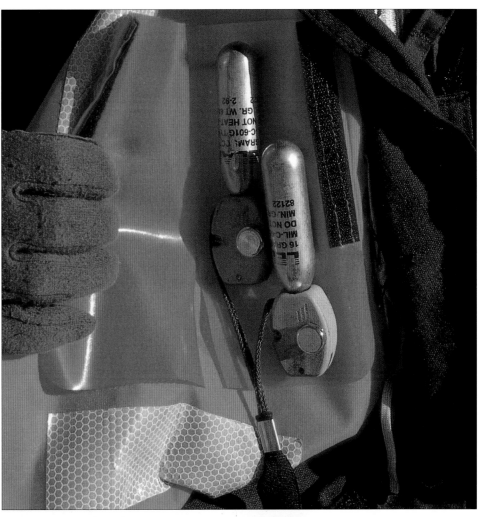

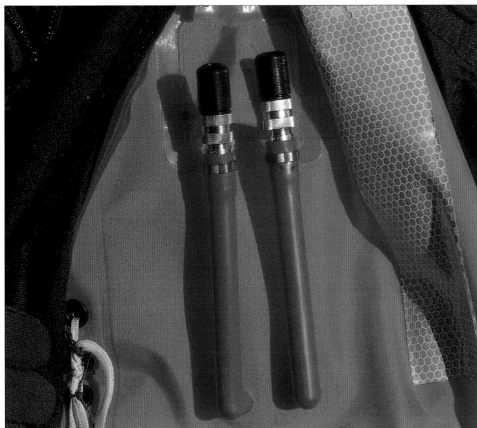

Two carbon dioxide cartridges inflate the Coast Guard life preserver at the tug of a lanyard, but there are oral inflation tubes as back-up.

(Left) Female aircrew member serving with the HH-65A Dolphin unit wearing the Coast Guard's blue flight suit.

(Right) Fred Fijn is a Coast Guard rescue swimmer, a job with "real world" hazards which include jumping into the bone-numbingly cold North Pacific to save lives. Unlike most US military aviation attire, Fred's flight gear is designed for high visibility.

(Left) Fred Fijn's buoyancy compensator, with the contents of the pouch on top; the PRC-90 is waterproof, and allows the rescue swimmer to keep in contact with the helicopter hovering overhead.

(Left, below & opposite)
USAF Sgt.Bey is an ALSE
specialist with an F-111
Aardvark squadron of the
27th Tactical Fighter Wing at
Cannon AFB, New Mexico.
The HGU-55/P Combat
Edge helmets are inspected
and cleaned after each
flight, and periodically
disassembled and inspected
in more detail.

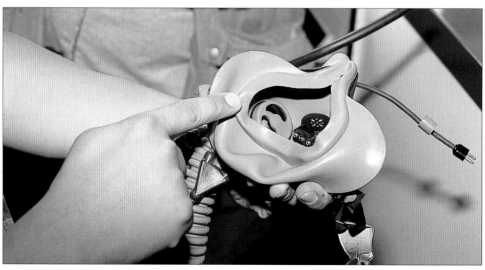

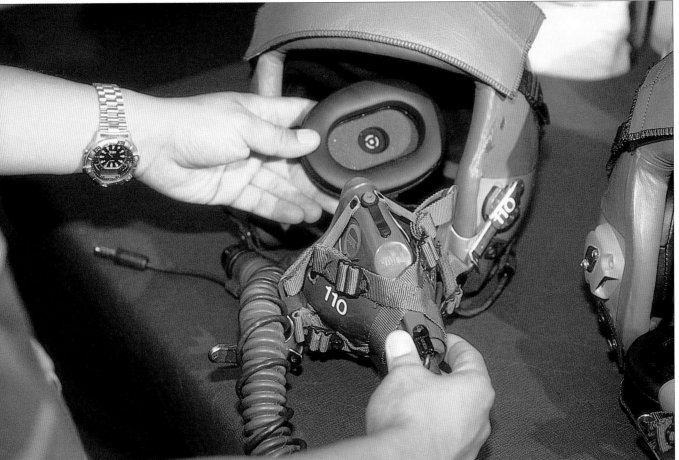

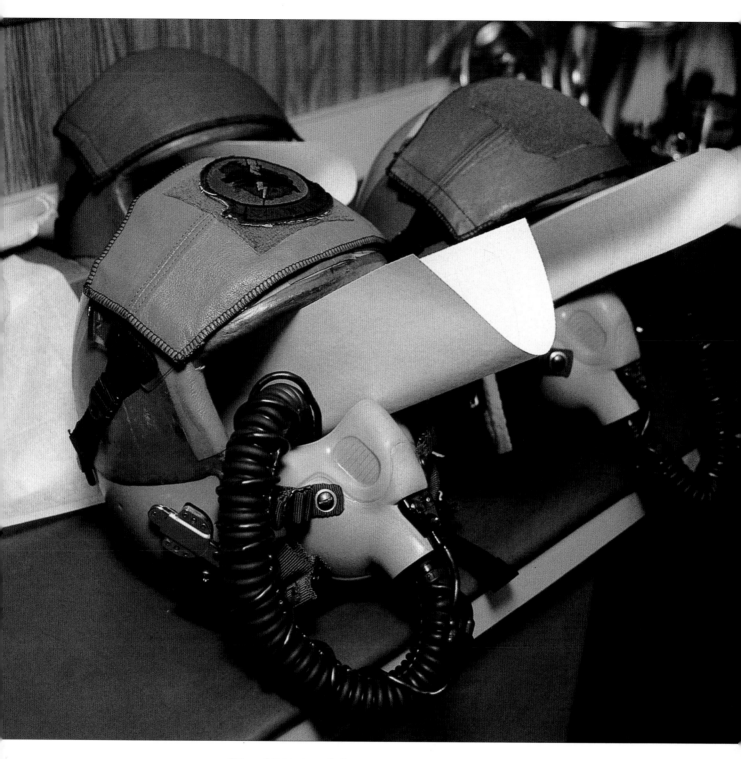

(Above) HGU-55/P helmets with MBU-12/P oxygen masks, freshly inspected and certified by the ALSE shop, wait to be returned to the rightful owners to whose skulls their liners have been individually moulded.

(Right) USAF Captain Dan Holmes, at his place of business. Note the more upright position of the ejection seat in the F-15E Strike Eagle as compared with that in the F-16; and note also the parachute risers attached from the seat 'chute stowage to Capt. Holmes's harness.

(Aove) At Seymour Johnson AFB, 1991, Captain Ray Toth of the 336th TFS, 4th TFW demonstrates the proper fit of the MBU-5/P oxygen mask: tight enough to prevent leakage. The mask may be hot, sticky, heavy and uncomfortable; but it provides essential oxygen in a hostile environment, houses the microphone which is your only link with the rest of the human race, and protects your lower face if you have to punch out into 500-knot wind blast.

(Right) TSgt.Troy Arce of the 129th Rescue Group wears a recycled and heavily modified HGU-55 helmet previously issued to a USAF fighter pilot. The visor assembly has been removed, and the microphone and communications wiring normally used on helicopter helmets have been installed. The low profile, originally intended to reduce air loads on a pilot's head during ejection, makes for less resistance when TSgt.Arce sticks his head out of the helicopter door into the slipstream to observe ground conditions.

Lt.C. Doug Munday

1. PUSH BUTTON TO OPEN DOOR
2. PULL RING OUT 6 FEET TO
   JETTISON CANOPY

(Left & below) In the cockpit of his F-16 LTC Bill Gore of the 144th FW prepares for take-off; the slightly reclining angle of the ACES II ejection seat somewhat reduces the effects of high positive G-loads as compared with the seat installation in other fighters. Note, at the left side of his HGU-55/P(CE) helmet, the hose connecting to a bladder in the nape section of the helmet. The bladder is automatically pressurized during high-G manoeuvers, tensioning the mask against the face to prevent leakage.

(Previous pages) US Navy F-14 Tomcat pilots flying out of NAS Fallon show off variously decorated HGU-33 helmets - distinguishable by the internal attachment of the visors, with a central slot and knob - in the gaudy days of the early 1990s. (Photos Robert Genat)

(Below) A Navy A-6 Intruder crew from CV-64 wearing HGU-33s.

(Right) This Navy F/A-18 Hornet crew with VFA-305, photographed in 1992 at NAS Point Mugu, show off a popular post-"Desert Storm" fashion in camouflaged helmet covers. (Photo Robert Genat)

(**Far left**) US Marine OV-10 Bronco crewmen from VMO-2 strike the corniest "flyboy" pose in the book. Once again, note the full anti-gravity wardrobe and survival kit worn by these prop-jockeys, who may find themselves twisting and turning just above the weeds to avoid ground fire; for the same reason, helmet covers in BDU material are popular.
(Photo Robert Genat)

(**Left**) This AH-1 Cobra attack helicopter pilot from the US Army's 7th Infantry Division wears a modified SPH-4 helmet with brackets for night vision goggles and a sighting system for the 20mm cannon.

(**Below**) What's wrong with this picture? Well, for one thing the observer on the left is wearing an SPH-4 helicopter crew helmet for a flight in an OV-2 Mohawk, an aircraft equipped with ejection seats. Note that the SPH-4 has receivers for an oxygen mask - and a boom mike. If you can talk on a boom mike while wearing an oxygen mask, you must have a REAL loud voice.

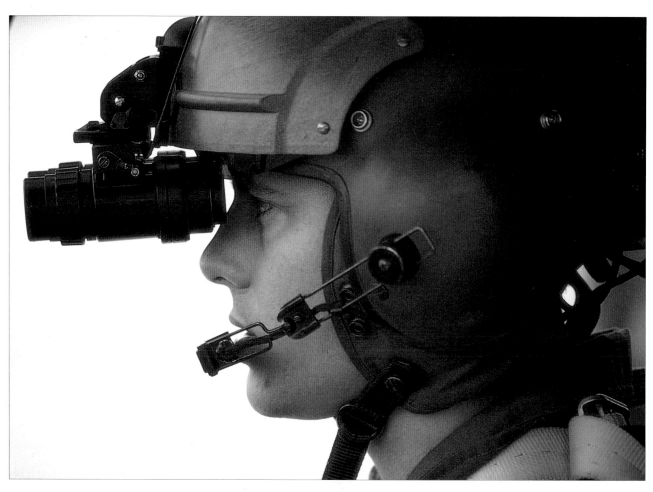

(Left top) Profile view of the ANVIS-6 NVG (night vision goggles), mounted on the modified SPH-4 helmet of an Army OV-58D pilot. When the NVG were introduced to the helicopter community they revolutionized the conduct of operations - even though they gave pilots a real headache. The weight distribution was one serious problem, the security of the mount another; both have been largely solved with current helmet and bracket designs.

(Left bottom) SPH-4 with NVG fitted; this and the profile view show the clearance between the night vision goggles and the pilot's face. The goggles are only for looking out of the cockpit; the pilot has to glance down under them to see his instruments and charts. While it took a while to work out the bugs, NVG technology has now improved to the point where US Army aviators can steam along at full throttle just above the treetops on the darkest and stormiest nights - and almost never hit anything.

(Below) A Cobra from the 7th Infantry Division prowls the training area of Fort Ord, California. The linkage for the gunner's helmet target designation system is visible at the top of the canopy.

(**Above**) No, this Cobra gunner hasn't taken a serious hit during an attack run against a hostile country club; the tennis ball is up there to prevent the bracket on his helmet from damaging the canopy before the linkage is attached.

(**Right**) LTC Rick Rife commands a US Army AH-64 Apache attack helicopter battalion in Korea; during the Gulf War he led an Apache unit in combat. His huge, heavy helmet - unique to the Apache - is the extraordinary-looking IHADSS, which offers him the same kind of "head-up display" of navigation and weapons information as enjoyed by jet fighter pilots. The helmet's "slaving" system also allows Col.Rife to aim the Apache's 30mm cannon simply by turning his head to look at the target.

Integrated Helmet
And Display Sight Subsystem

(Right) CWO4 John Cooney, a Vietnam combat veteran still serving and still flying, photographed in his place of work. The Apache crews' IHADSS has to be treated with some care, as its components are fairly fragile and easily damaged; the wiring loom for the optical relay tube alone costs $4500.

(Below left & right) Close-ups of Col.Rife's IHADSS. The monocle in front of the right eye is the screen on which "head-up" information is projected via the optical relay tube by his cheek, so that he does not have to look down at his instruments during combat manoeuvers. This tube assembly is a real hazard in a crash, and some Apache pilots have suffered severe facial injuries on impact.

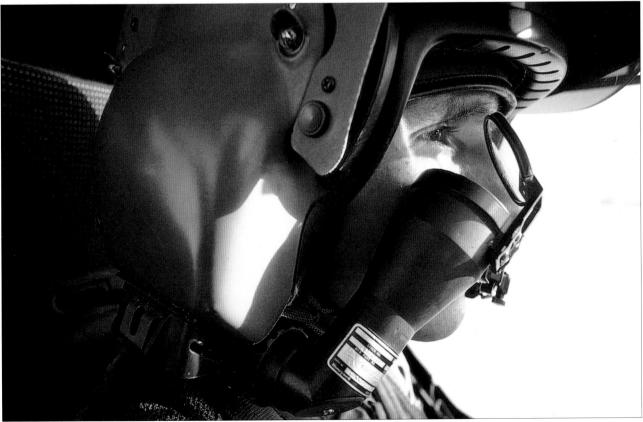

(Above) The huge size of the IHADSS helps distribute the extra weight of the optical relay tube on the right side; but it undeniably gives the Apache pilot a weird, "Star Wars alien" appearance.

US Coast Guard

(Above) The pilot of a US Coast Guard HH-65A Dolphin chopper (the French Aerospatiale SA.365N) straps in; he wears the standard SPH-4 helmet and the USCG's trim blue flight suit. (Photo Robert Genat)

(Far left) USCG flight suit, and a helmet adorned with a patriotic - and strictly non-regulation - visor cover motif. (Photo Robert Genat)

(Left) Gentex developed this SPH-5CG helmet specially for the Coast Guard; the ANVIS-6 night vision goggles get plenty of use during the Guard's over-water missions after dark, whether they are searching for mariners in distress or for more sinister trade.

(Below) Profile view of the ANVIS-6 NVG mounted on the SPH-5CG helmet. The helmet has dual visors - clear and dark gray - mounted on a composite shell with an energy-absorbing polystyrene liner; the M87 boom microphone has a little "lip light" attached.

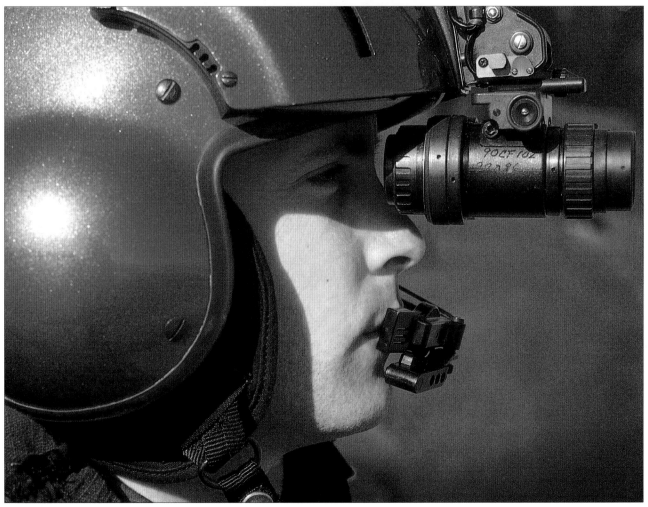

(Top) Detail of the battery pack for the ANVIS-6 attached to the SPH-5CG.

NASA ER-2 Pilot Protective Assembly

(Below) The latest manifestation of the legendary U-2 ultra-long range, ultra-high altitude reconnaissance aircraft is NASA's ER-2 (though this venerable design is still in military use, and one was recently lost in a tragic take-off accident while operating from Great Britain over Bosnia). NASA pilot Doyle Krumery will be imprisoned in the Pilot Protective Assembly and GNS-1031 helmet for another four or five hours.

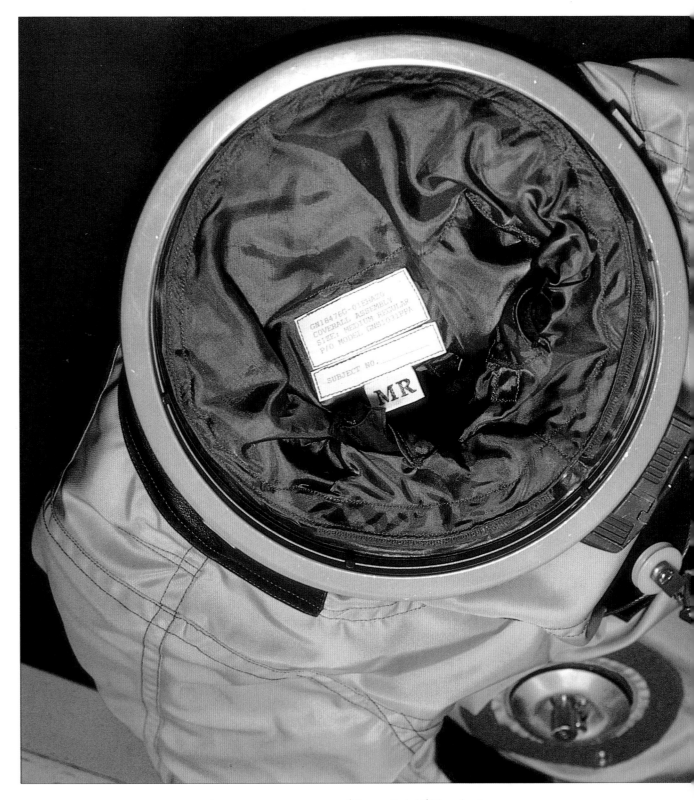

GN18476C-01ER47C
COVERALL ASSEMBLY
SIZE: MEDIUM REGULAR
P/O MODEL GNS1011PPA

SUBJECT NO.

MR

(Above & right) You don't exactly buy a PPA off the rack, even if you are a Medium/Regular; each rig is custom-fitted to the individual pilot by a team of support specialists.

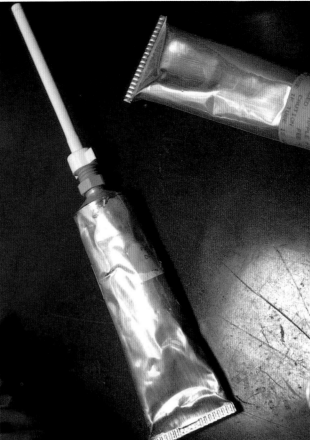

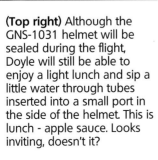

(Top right) Although the GNS-1031 helmet will be sealed during the flight, Doyle will still be able to enjoy a light lunch and sip a little water through tubes inserted into a small port in the side of the helmet. This is lunch - apple sauce. Looks inviting, doesn't it?

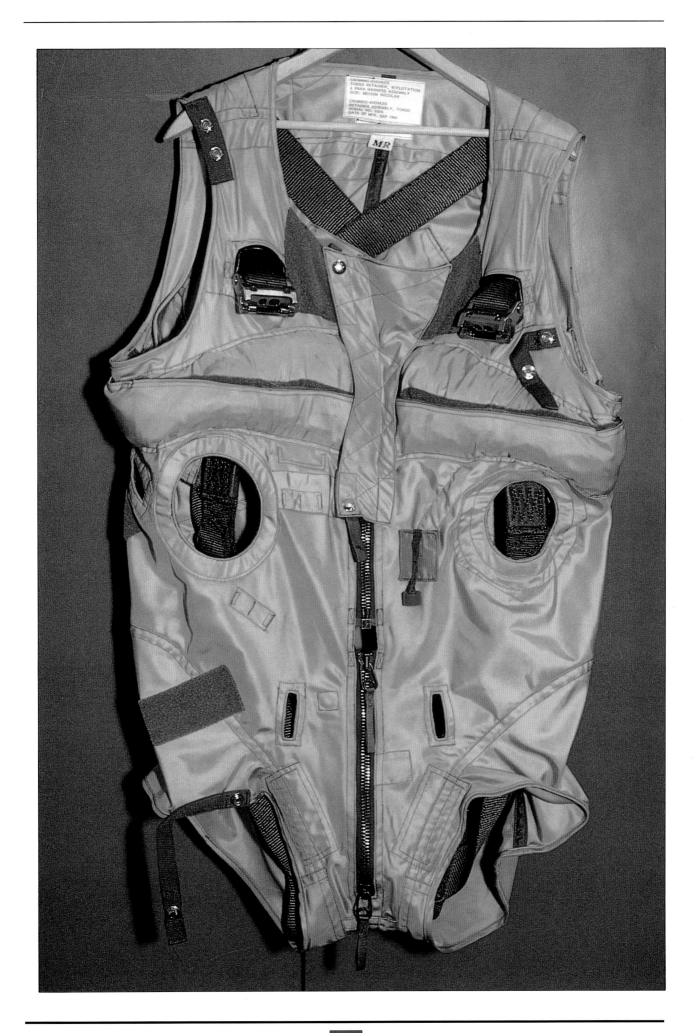

(Previous page, below left & right) The ER-2 pilot's parachute harness includes an accessory garment unique to the high altitude mission - the Torso Retention Assembly with Flotation and Harness. Quick-release fittings poke through from the harness worn underneath; a flotation device is stowed just below the buckles.

(Bottom, & opposite) In place of "speed jeans", for flights at the threshold of space these ER-2 pilots wear a full pressure suit; here Doyle Krumery's Pilot Protective Assembly is being carefully checked for leaks before his mission.

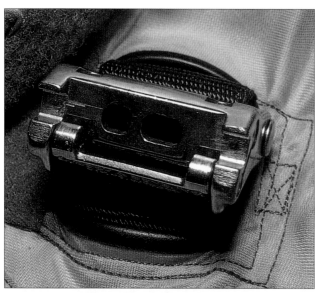

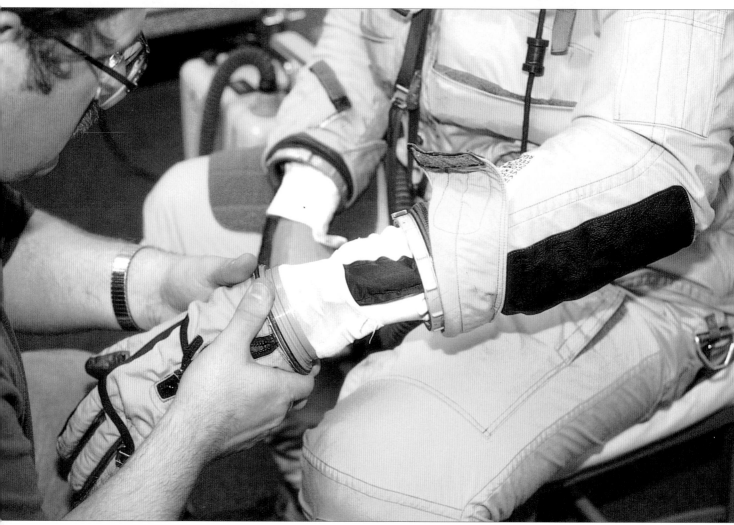

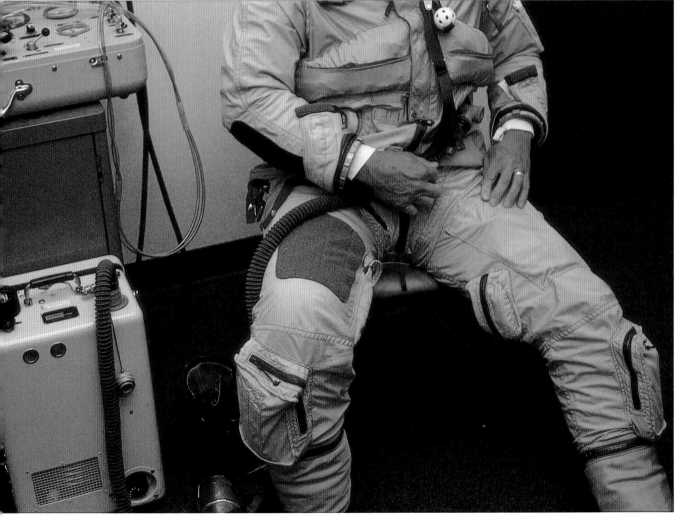

(**Left & right**) With about half an hour to go before launch, Krumery heads out to the flight line accompanied by his trusty attendant James Sokolik. Sokolik carries the portable system which provides cooling for the suit - without it the pilot would quickly overheat.

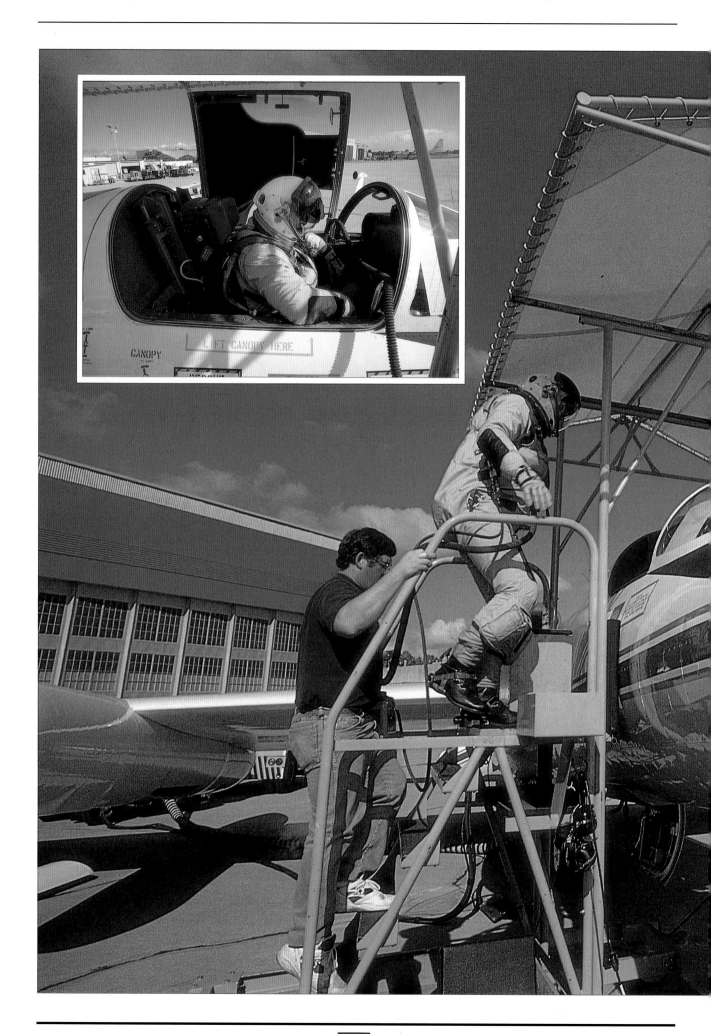

(Previous two pages)
Strapped in, powered up, his suit pressurized, Doyle Krumery is ready to fire up and launch the ER-2. Average mission length is four hours - a long time in a full pressure suit almost identical to the space suits worn by astronauts - and some can be considerably longer.

(Right & below) Very few pilots qualify to fly the ER-2, so these are rare prizes for the patch collectors. Even the life support crew have their own patch; the skunk in the suit is a tribute to the ER-2's heritage as a product of Kelly Johnson's legendary "Skunk Works" in the Lockheed facility at Burbank, California.

"PJs"

(Right) Master Sergeant Tim Williams, a veteran "PJ" - parachute rescue jumper - assigned to the 129th Rescue Group, suits up in the locker room before a flight. Apart from five jumps into the North Pacific Ocean in the course of serious off-shore rescue missions, Tim has participated in over 75 "real world" land rescues in the USA and United Kingdom (including many in Wales, a rugged land of black rocks, treeless mountains and incessant rain).

(Left) The kit used by military aircrews varies considerably. This locker contains parachutes and other equipment issued to the 129th Rescue Group, an Air Force CSAR outfit.

(**Left & below**) Assisted by TSgt.Troy Arce, MSgt.Willams dons the MTIX free-fall parachute. This is a high performance ram-air canopy system providing the rescue jumper with tremendous control and a long glide ratio. Normal jump altitude is 13,000 feet; PJs use this canopy with surface winds up to 17 miles per hour.

(Right) Since his job is to jump out of airplanes, MSgt.Williams carries just about the biggest survival kit around. The rucksack contains drugs, surgical tools and medical supplies; Tim will be the first, and maybe the only rescuer to reach a casualty for some time before they can be extracted, and he is qualified to perform many kinds of life-saving medical procedures.

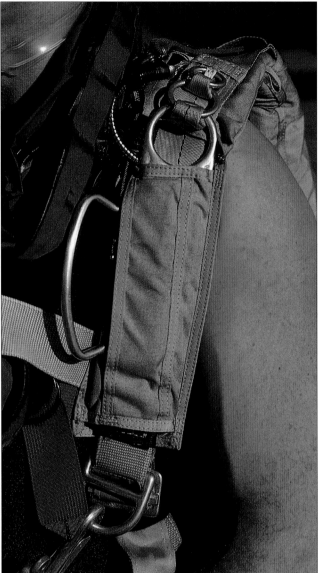

(Above) Detail of one of the two ripcord D-handles on the MTIX rig - the backpack contains both the main canopy and the reserve.

(Left) The dive knife is not standard issue, but is acquired by virtually all Air Force and Coast Guard rescue swimmers.

CHAPTER 4
Survival Kit

The immediate business of escaping from a crippled airframe and falling safely to earth naturally occupies the pilot's full attention; but it is only the first step in survival. The difficulty of overcoming the challenges which confront downed aircrew from the moment when they roll over and stand up is encapsulated by the following account (reprinted from *Flightfax*, September 1994:)

It was a routine night recon into the mountains, and the accident crew was Chalk 3 in a flight of four AH-64s flying in staggered-right formation. They had been airborne for 32 minutes when they encountered unforecasted snow showers. The air mission commander announced that he was starting a 180-degree left turn to return to station. As Chalk 3 turned left to exit the weather, it crashed at the top of a 7,000-foot mountain. The following is an account by CW4 Franklin C. Harrison and CW2 Daniel R.Smee, Company A, 2d Battalion, 229th Aviation Regiment, [operating out of] Fort Rucker, AL, of what happened after the crash, and the crew members' actions until they were rescued more than two and a half very cold hours later.

CW4 Harrison's account:

"I'm alive" was my first thought when the aircraft stopped rocking from side to side. I tried to call Dan, my front seat pilot. No answer. During the crash sequence his helmet mike cord had come unplugged. He was trying to call me, I was trying to call him, and neither of us could hear the other. Obviously, some very unpleasant thoughts about each other's condition flashed through our minds in those first few seconds.

I immediately shut down the engines. As I was exiting the aircraft I saw Dan. When the aircraft started vibrating and rocking from side to side, Dan had ducked down as low as he could in the seat to avoid any rotor blades that might come through the cockpit. He could hear the fuel escaping from the ruptured auxiliary tank that had been mounted on the right wing, and he climbed out through the opening where his left canopy had been broken away.

Much relieved to see each other, we quickly moved about 25 feet away from the aircraft and did a quick appraisal of our physical condition. I thought I had broken my left arm on the armor seat during the impact. However, on examination we found that it wasn't broken, just banged up pretty good. Dan had a small cut on his right cheek and scratches on his right arm. All in all, we were in great shape considering what had just happened.

I was told when I started flying helicopters in 1968 that "if it's not on you at the time of a crash, chances are you won't get it out of the aircraft." We were lucky. There was no postcrash fire, and we were able to return to the aircraft and retrieve our Gore-Tex parkas and sleeping bags from the wreckage. By then it was snowing very hard on the mountaintop and the wind was blowing at 20 knots or more. We heard an aircraft circling to our south clear of the snow shower. It was our lead aircraft - the company commander. I attempted to contact them on my PRC-90 survival radio to let them know we were down safe but the aircraft was destroyed. I got no reply, so I changed over to the beacon mode. Still no reply.

We assessed our situation, and realized that due to weather conditions on the mountain it was going to be difficult for a rescue aircraft to get to us. Knowing that we would not be rescued where we were until hours later when the weather cleared, we decided to climb down to the valley floor about 700 feet below to better our chances of being picked up sooner. We did a quick inventory of what we had and decided to take our sleeping bags and wear our survival vests under our Gore-Tex parkas. I had two flashlights and Dan had one. I was wearing my Nomex gloves; Dan had a pair of inserts he could pull on over his Nomex gloves. Prior to flight school, Dan had been an Army Ranger School instructor with extensive mountain

(Left) The little signal mirror is found in virtually all survival kits, normally attached to a short length of "dummy cord" to prevent loss. Although it is just about the most "low tech" item of gear you can carry, it has saved members of this officer's unit when the PRC-90 and smoke signals did not work.

open, and out he climbed. We walked away from the aircraft and assessed our physical damage. Outside of a couple of scratches and bumps, we were basically intact.

We could hear an aircraft circling to the south and tried to reach them on our PRC-90s, but were unable to establish voice communication. Frank went to beacon. Still no luck. We were fortunate to have brought our Gore-Tex parkas and our sleeping bags with us, because we knew how cold it could get in the desert at night. We gathered our gear and secured our helmets and kneeboards along with the rest of our gear in our bags and placed them away from the aircraft, because we knew the accident board was going to need them. Still unable to raise voice with the other aircraft, we then decided to proceed down the hill.

The climb down was interesting, to say the least. I had been in snow before, but never on top of a mountain in the middle of the night. I knew that this was going to be good. Our objective was to make our way down to where the weather was better and the terrain conducive to safe rescue. For an "old guy" Frank surprised me: he really didn't have any serious problems keeping up on the descent. The going was slow and the distance down to the next drop was hard to judge due to the darkness and the snow. We would drop our sleeping bags from one level to the next and use them as a reference to judge distance. Slow, but it worked extremely well.

When we reached a streambed we followed it to the valley floor; and then we decided to build a fire and wait there for someone to pick us up. The weather was still

(Above) Major Ryan Orian gets his bearings; the compass is luminous and can be used night or day. When flying over known hostile territory, aircrew are briefed on the position and appearance of landmarks which are given codenames. The idea is not that downed pilots should try to make their way towards these, but rather that they should use them as reference points for distances and directions when they succeed in making radio contact with CSAR aircraft.

(Right) Close-up of the snap link, for attaching to a rescue hoist, normally fitted to the harness worn by Navy and Marine aircrews. The angle-head flashlight is used by all the services; with its red lens, it is useful in the cockpit when a chart or kneeboard needs to be consulted after dark without ruining the pilot's night vision.

bad, and we were not sure if it would permit a pickup that night or not. In my survival training I had never had a hard time starting a fire when needed. Not now. First the radio hadn't worked, although we had just checked it a few days prior, and now the matches in our survival vests were inop. Our luck seemed to be running kind of thin. Magnesium firestarter was the next weapon of choice. My fingers were pretty cold from the climb down, and we were both wet to the bone. A fire was sure going to feel good, just as soon as I could get one going. Well, the magnesium didn't work either. No matter how hard we tried to build a windbreak, the wind was too strong for it to contain the shavings.

Finally our luck began to change: an Air Force search-and-rescue aircraft had seen the sparks of the firestarter, and was able to visually home in on our position. When we heard them we were able to establish contact with them for pickup, although we still didn't have two-way communication.

These events took place in a period of two and a half hours; two and a half long, miserable hours, and plenty of time to think about [the importance of] pre-mission planning...If we had not brought our parkas and our sleeping bags it is very likely that we could have been cold-weather casualties to some degree. As it turned out, the SAR aircraft had made two previous attempts to reach the crash scene and had been forced to turn back. On their third attempt they had spotted the spark of light as we were desperately trying to get a fire started.

Frank and I both have a better appreciation for the survival vest than we did before the accident. I know that if I'm going to have to wear it, I'm going to ensure that things work as advertised. Regardless of current inspection dates and the presence of matches and other required items, if they don't work or you don't know how to use them, they can't be of much help to you when you really need them. From now on, I'll check everything.

Tools for Survival

As "war stories" like this one show, when things go bad on a military flight, they go bad in a big way. One of the things early aviators learned through sad experience is that the only survival tools you are likely to have in a real emergency are the ones you are wearing when the wings start to fall off the aircraft.

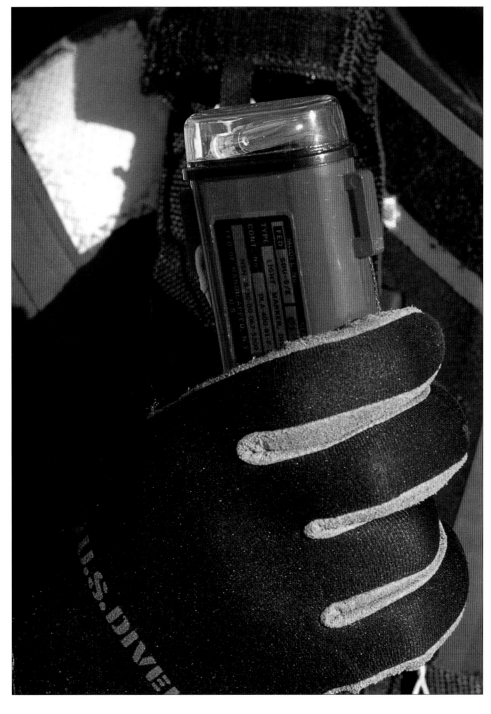

(Left) Standard equipment for virtually all military aircrew in all the services is the SDU-5E strobe, usually tied securely into a pocket on the right front of the vest. The batteries last for about eight hours.

(Right) The Coast Guard has plenty of use for the SDU-5E, especially when rescue swimmers like Fred Fijn have to jump into the Pacific Ocean, day or night. The strobe usually has Velcro attached to one side so that it can be fixed to a mating patch on the helmet, leaving the swimmer's hands free.

The specific items of gear vary with the branch of service, the aircraft type, the particular unit, and even with the individual aircrew member. You won't find a HEED bottle in the vest contents of very many US Army UH-60 helicopter crew members, for example, but virtually every US Navy crew flying the SH-60 (the naval equivalent of the UH-60) will have one stowed neatly in the front of the survival vest, ready for a trip to the surface when the helicopter submerges.

Vest, SRU-21/P
Survival vests have been worn by US Army aviators at least since World War II; my father, a navigator on B-24 Liberators, wore one quite similar to those still issued today, fifty years later. It a concept that hasn't needed a lot of improvement; the original idea was that, in an emergency,

you don't have time to collect the things you may need to escape, evade and survive. A bail-out is a "come as you are" event. If you are wearing the essentials when the order to abandon the aircraft comes, you'll have them on the ground - otherwise you are out of luck.

The current US Army survival vest design is designated SRU-21/P, and comes in two sizes, Large and Small. It is made from "raschel" knit nylon, with laces in back to adjust the fit, and a zippered front. Those laces can be really important - the vest can be worn with body armor, a parachute harness and a life-preserver, but not without some adjustments. Fully loaded, with pistol and knife and other items, it weighs about seven and a half pounds. That might not sound like much, but it will feel more like 70 pounds after you've worn the vest, the armor, a helmet and a pistol for a long mission.

(**Above**) One obscure and dull-looking item stowed in the vest can make the difference between life and death in a hurry - a tourniquet strap.

(**Right**) This stainless steel pocket knife can be found in just about every survival kit, large or small; it is usually secured by a lanyard.

(**Far right**) Typical of the many varieties of issue or personally acquired survival knives carried by virtually all military aircrew.

The correct way to get the vest on is to first put on your body armor; then the LPU-10/P life-preserver, if that's required for an over-water flight; your mission commander will indicate during the mission briefing if you need to wear the armor or the life-preserver. Once both are fitted, pull on the survival vest - it will be *much* more comfortable if you pull the bladders through the openings for your arms, as intended by the designers. Finally, if you need one, the parachute goes on over all this. If you can adjust the parachute harness to fit both snugly and comfortably over all that stuff, it will be a military miracle.

Pockets on the vest accommodate a wide range of survival tools and supplies, some standard issue and some optional. One of the best is the little radio mentioned several times already in this text.

Rescue Radio PRC-90

If anybody ever asks you that dumb, age-old question, "what one thing would you like to have if you were marooned on a desert island?", answer "a PRC-90!" This little radio, in all its permutations, has saved large numbers of US military aviators - it is a combat-proven device, and when life turns sour on you there is a good likelihood that it will..." get your ass out of Dodge City.

It is about the size of a paperback book, about as heavy

as a pistol. If you do find yourself marooned on that desert island, pull the radio out of its pocket in your vest, on the left side right in front. The telescopic antenna extends just like the one on portable stereo radios; pull it all the way out before turning the radio on. If you are shot down behind enemy lines, trying to evade the bad guys, a little earphone will keep the radio from advertising your location.

A rotary switch in the middle of the radio is clearly marked with four positions: OFF, Voice 282.8, Voice MCW 243.0, and BCN 243.0. The battery is good for only 14 hours of operation, and reception and transmission is pretty much limited to line-of-sight, so conserve the battery by leaving the radio switched off unless you see an aircraft overhead or are pretty sure one is in the area - sometimes you can hear a plane without being able to see it.

When you're ready to call for help, turn the switch to BCN; hold the antenna vertically for best signal propagation (do *not* point it at the aircraft), and say your prayers. The beacon signal will be picked up by nearly every airplane in range, and its whooping sound will be understood in every cockpit as a call for help. There is a good chance that an aircraft which hears the signal will divert from its course, home on the signal, and orbit your position. Be sure to leave the beacon on if you think aircraft are in

And what do you say when the SAR chopper materializes over the hill? There are two options. The first is what you are *supposed* to say: "CQ, RESCUE CRAFT, CQ, CQ, CQ. OVER." They are supposed to call back: "ROGER, ROGER, ROGER, READ YOU FIVE BY FIVE," or more likely," READ YOU BROKEN AND INTERMITTENT." In a combat environment you will certainly be required to authenticate yourself, probably with a call sign, a code word, or some personal information like your previous squadron.

You call back, "ROGER, ROGER. CREW STATUS FOLLOWS... "; then you report on physical status, missing crew members, any emergency logistical requirements (like water, food, or medical supplies), concluding, "ROGER, OUT." Although this is the way it is supposed to go, real life emotions tend to get in the way and actual transmissions tend to be more chaotic, particularly when the bad guys are closing in; "GET ME OUT OF HERE!" is a recurring theme. Just remember, don't shout... and don't beg (although plenty of people do).

HEED 3 Oxygen Bottle

A durable can of "spare air" that automatically starts when removed from the vest, the HEED 3 can be used upside down as well as right side up (unlike its predecessor the ESAS.) Also unlike the ESAS, it has a indicator to show if there is any air left in the tank.

A vivid example of the value of the HEED bottle was recounted (in *Approach* Magazine, August 1994, under the title "My Submarine Seasprite Ride") by Navy helicopter crewman Lieutenant E.Reed of squadron VT-27:

My HAC and I were returning from a flawless torp-drop exercise at the Pacific Missile Test Facilities off Kauai; the range monitor had commended us for one of the best ASW runs he had seen in months. We had eaten, debriefed, preflighted and were now headed for home. The SH-2F has an auto-blade track system that basically helps to maintain a smooth rotor track. However, as soon as we took off we began experiencing what is commonly called a one-vibration-per-revolution, or "one-per".

The HAC in the left seat decided to manually track the blades in flight, which is a common practice since the auto-tracking system occasionally gets squirrelly. Unable to get a smooth track like the one we had before leaving the range, we decided to give the auto system another shot. No sooner had we engaged the system than our worst nightmare began. The servo flap on one of the main rotor blades departed its main member, and the aircraft started vibrating violently - vertically and laterally. The vibrations were so bad that we were afraid the rotors would fail. Although we were only 1.5 miles from a paved airfield, the severity of the vibrations forced us to ditch. We autorotated, entering the water with zero ground speed.

As soon as we hit, the seats bottomed out and the front cockpit windows exploded. The helo immediately rolled right; I was under water, out of breath and inverted before I could realize this was the real thing. A SEAL chief taught me in "stupid swim" that "panic in the water is an irreversible process." I tried to maintain my composure as best I could with no air in my lungs and strapped to a piece of metal that had me upside down and sinking fast.

Our survival is a testament to the effectiveness of the Navy's water survival and emergency procedures training. I don't remember why, but the first thing I did was reach for my HEED bottle in my SV-2. After a couple of breaths, I felt completely at ease. I then quickly disconnected my cords and harness, and evacuated the aircraft. As I rose to the

range and trying to home on you; the direction-finding navigation systems in the plane will depend on a continuous signal to provide an accurate heading. Once you have company overhead you can switch from the beacon position to two-way voice on 243.0 or 282.8 MHz.

This procedure will work most of the time - you will probably have company when your aircraft goes down in flames, and your mates will probably know you're on the ground and will be looking for you. Sometimes, as in O'Grady's case, it's not that quick and simple; then you've got to ration the battery or you won't have any juice left when you need it. The SOP for battery conservation is as follows:
*Limit your transmissions to daylight for better signal propagation.
*Best range will typically be achieved at sunrise and sunset.
*Send a "mayday" or SOS once at sunrise, once at noon, once at sunset.
*For each of these three transmission periods, transmit for two minutes, then switch off for one minute; on for three minutes, then off for three minutes; then on for ten minutes.
*You will get the best range and reception from the highest terrain, so find a safe and secure hilltop if one is handy. The beacon setting uses the least power.

surface I was concerned about getting an air embolism, so I let my HEED bottle fall from my mouth, stroking and kicking my way upward for what seemed like an eternity. The subsequent rescue was quick and uneventful. The HEED bottle saved my life. I might not have been able to exit the aircraft without it. HEED gave me a second chance.

Mk 79 Pencil Flare Launcher

There are seven flares in a bandoleer, each of which lasts about four and a half seconds. The flare goes from 400 to 600 feet in the air, and can be seen from quite a distance.

Mk 13 Mod 0 Hand Held Signal Flare

The Mk 13 flare has a night end (identifiable by touch by its raised cap) which emits a brilliant red light; and a day end which puts out orange smoke. Each end lasts about 20 seconds.

SDU-5E Strobe Marker

"This is the best survival item in the vest," says Fred Fijn of the US Coast Guard. "It has already saved lives in the military. It cuts through fog really well - it's a very high powered light. It's also used by the rescue swimmer to signal to the helicopter that he's in trouble." The strobe is carried by virtually all aircrew, sometimes in the vest with a second one on a harness or elsewhere. Navy, Marine and Coast Guard pilots and crew use the SDU-5E a little differently from members of services who are less likely

(Above) Scraping a magnesium fire-starter with the survival knife will sometimes get the kindling going when matches have failed. With all the thought, expense and effort that have gone into providing aircrew with the most ingenious and sophisticated aids, the oldest wilderness imperative of all - starting a fire - can still sometimes make the difference between survival and a wretched, needless death.

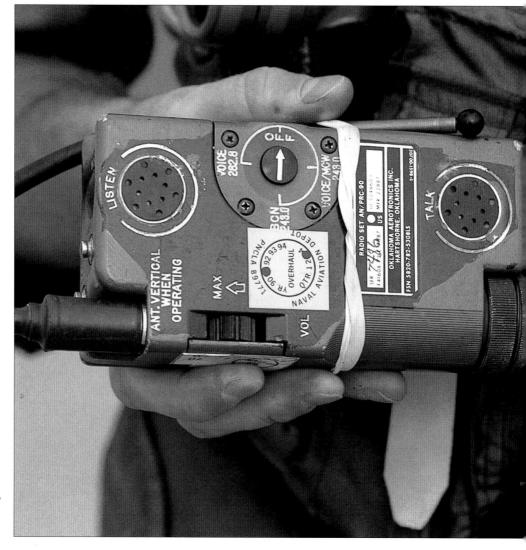

(Left) An older, "plain vanilla" version of the PRC-90 with Morse code capability on 243.0 Mhz - the "MCW" position on the selector switch. It has now been decided that so few personnel still know Morse that the capability is obsolete, and has been omitted from the current issue PRC-90-2 (see photos in Chapter One).

to fly over water. The former often Velcro the strobe so that it can be attached to the helmet or to the shoulder while swimming, leaving the hands free (it is not unknown for Army personnel to do the same, to leave their hands free for handling weapons.)

As we learned in Vietnam, getting the rescue chopper into your vicinity was sometimes the easy part of the problem. In many kinds of terrain, particularly in the jungle, a person is often virtually invisible from the air. Several devices were invented during the 1960s to remedy this problem, and one of the best is the Strobe Marker. You will find the SDU-5E in its own pocket, typically on the right front of the vest.

The strobe is totally waterproof and will function even under water. Flip the switch on the side of the strobe, and a very bright flash every five seconds will advertise your position to anybody with line-of-sight on you up to five miles away.

Of course, this is not always such a hot idea. The SDU-5 has two modifications to make it more helpful in a combat zone: the lens cover is now blue to keep the flash from looking like the muzzle flash from a weapon; and a little foam sleeve can be used to cover part of the lens to let you aim the flash up toward the rescue aircraft - they can see it, but the bad guys in the neighborhood can't.

(Above) These little cartridges, of which seven are provided stowed neatly in this plastic bandoleer, fit the M-201 flare gun - a miniature launcher that looks like a small flashlight. When fired the little rocket soars up to about 1,100 feet, trailing red fire, before bursting with a flash that should be visible for several miles (assuming anyone is looking in the right direction, of course...)

(Left) The Mk 13 combination smoke/flare signal, of which several are typically stowed in the seat pack survival kit, is designed for both day and night use. The bumps on the cover cap allow you to identify the flare end by touch on the darkest night. Pop the cap off to expose a metal pull-ring, and yank it to initiate the device. The result will be a bright red flare, visible for several miles at night. The opposite end works in the same way but produces bright orange smoke for daytime signalling. After the multiple shocks to the mind and body suffered during a high-speed ejection and a parachute descent and landing, a surprising number of people have difficulty handling this device correctly, and waste the flare by day or the smoke by night.

Signal Kit, Foliage Penetrating M-201

An alternative method of marking your position is with the little flare gun; in the Army version of the vest this kit goes in a pocket at the back on the right side. The launcher and seven red flare cartridges fit together in a little kit. If you need to use it, attach one of the cartridges to the launcher, point the device straight up, pull the spring-loaded knob down, then release it quickly. The gun will fire, shooting the flare up (through three layers of jungle canopy, if necessary) to an altitude of 1,100

(Left) PRC-90 in use. The earphone is an important element of the system under combat conditions, when even the sound of the sidetone static coming from the earpiece of the radio can give away your position to hostile searchers.

(Below) This little can of "spare air" is the Helicopter Emergency Egress Device - the legendary HEED bottle. When your helicopter lands

in the drink, rolls over, and thrashes itself to death while sinking rapidly into the freezing black depths, you are supposed to remove this from your vest, rotate the knob, and stuff it in your mouth while unstrapping yourself, finding your way out the door, and making a break for the surface. As unlikely as it sounds, the HEED bottle works, and has saved many lives.

feet. With a burn time of about nine seconds, the flare is visible for about three miles during the day and ten miles at night.

Mirror, Mk 3

Another indispensable item in the well-dressed aviator's formal attire is the signal mirror Mk 3 or one of its variants - several models are issued, and some fliers buy one of the excellent commercial models available on the market. The mirror may have some limitations; but the batteries never run out, you can't use up its ammunition, and anybody can use one. All of the signal mirrors have some kind of window in the middle of the silvered surface.

If you hold the mirror in one hand and manoeuver the device a bit you will quickly discover the bright spot of light reflected by the sun; now, peep through the little window until you can see the bright reflected sun spot. You can now slowly adjust the mirror's angle to aim the reflection across a wide portion of the sky. While it only works in daylight, and is even more "line-of-sight" than the PRC-90, its flash is visible to an aircraft at 10,000 feet up to 30 miles away.

Knife, Folding

Nearly all survival kits contain the standard US-issue pocket knife, a simple five-bladed model made entirely from stainless steel with a large and a small knife blade, a can opener, a screwdriver, and an awl. "This is a basic survival item," one Coast Guard rescue swimmer told me. "You REALLY don't want to have this kicking around in your life raft out in the ocean, so one person will collect all the knives and anything else that can puncture the raft, and he will maintain custody of those knives as long as we are in the raft."

Pistol

There may be a few old .38 caliber revolvers still being issued by some units, but nearly every American aviator flying combat missions will carry the Beretta 9mm semi-automatic pistol in a holster on the left rear of the vest. A spare magazine, sometimes loaded with tracer ammunition for signalling, is sometimes stowed in one of the pockets of the vest.

The pistol is a much-maligned weapon, particularly among aircrew who very seldom have serious need for one. In fact it is a lot more accurate and effective than it usually gets credit for - in trained hands. It can be used for hunting as well as for protection. Many US fliers used their pistols to ward off capture in the jungles of Vietnam. But there are hazards attached to the pistol, too: once you start shooting, the other guys will know where you are. They are usually more heavily armed, better trained marksmen, and - if you shoot at them - much less likely to treat you in a relaxed manner when they close in on your lair. Capt.Scott O'Grady didn't even bother to load his pistol until just before his rescue. At least one USAF aviator, safe and sound on the ground after being forced to eject during a training flight over a wilderness area, became so panicked and depressed by his plight that he used his M1911 .45 pistol to blow his brains out - shortly before the rescue party found him.

(Above) The USAF search and rescue crews have a combat mission, and dress accordingly, complete with a pistol in their vests for those occasions when they may encounter unfriendlies on the surface at close quarters. The 9mm Beretta is standard issue these days; this "PJ" prefers a stainless steel .45 Colt, locked and loaded. Most combat aircrew will carry pistols in their survival vests; but there are escape-and-evasion situations when they are best advised to leave it there - its value is sometimes more psychological than practical.

CHAPTER 5
Ejection Seats

It's hard to imagine now, but the concept of permitting aircrew to abandon a sinking airship was once a matter of some debate. During World War I American aviators flew into combat without parachutes, partly because some commanders believed pilots would chose to bail out at the first sign of damage rather than fly a recoverable aircraft back to base. The result of this policy was that lots of pilots went down with the ship, in flames. Not until 1920 were US military aviators required to carry and, if necessary, use parachutes.

Up to and during World War II a flier could hope to depart a multi-seat airplane by climbing out of a hatch or through the bomb bay. Always assuming that the crewman was not seriously injured, and that the aircraft was not spinning or falling in an extreme attitude, the relatively leisurely pace of the bombers of the era made such escapes at least theoretically practical. (Under combat conditions, of course, stricken aircraft seldom flew straight and level for long enough for the large crews of those days to make it out the hatches before fire,

explosion, mid-air break-up or the paralysing centrifugal effect of a spin reduced their chances of survival to nil. It was tragically rare for all ten 'chutes to be seen blossoming in the wake of a falling Fortress or Liberator.)

If given the necessary time and altitude, the pilots of even 300-knot-plus fighters like the P-51 Mustang could usually slow down their wrecked ships sufficiently to make it possible to climb over the side - or at least to pop the canopy off, roll inverted, release their lap belt and helmet leads, and simply fall out, praying that they would miss the tailplane. But not always, even then; and as speeds increased, air-loads on crew climbing out into the slipstream began to prevent egress. Then, with the advent of jets and their much higher airspeeds, conventional bail-outs began to be impractical or impossible.

(Below) The ejection seat for the Lockheed ER-2 is a custom model unique to that aircraft, but shares many components and systems with other fast movers from the Skunk Works. This view shows the right hand side; note the lap belt attachment, oxygen system components, yellow emergency seat release handle, and fiberglass pack beneath containing survival items and emergency oxygen.

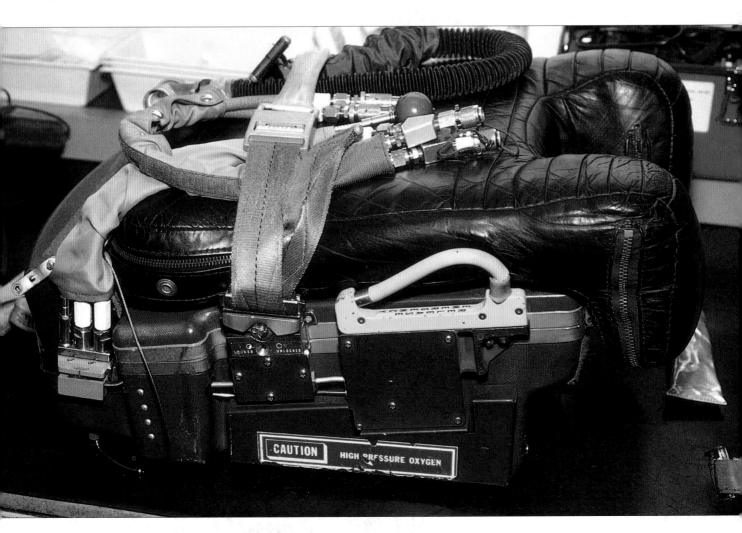

CAUTION   HIGH PRESSURE OXYGEN

(Above) ER-2 seat: riser attachments and D-handle for the parachute.

Right after the war Army Air Force technicians collected examples of ejection seats already in service - the J-21 seat from Sweden, and the Heinkel He 162 seat used in German high performance aircraft. Both patterns, along with much captured data, formed the foundation for the first US design. It was tested on 17 August 1946, with First Sergeant Lawrence Lambert in the hot seat; he has the dubious honour of being the first American to eject from an aircraft in flight. After further refinement the design entered service. The first emergency use occurred on 8 August 1949 when a US Navy pilot punched out of a dying McDonnell F2H-1 Banshee fighter. Just three weeks later the US Air Force christened the seat when a North American F-86 Sabrejet went out of control and the pilot ejected.

Surviving an Ejection
Modern ejection seats will save a pilot in most, but not all, emergencies. Survival depends largely on having enough time for the seat's parachute system to deploy completely - and often that time simply isn't available. Many emergencies happen on "short final" or take-off, or during low altitude manoeuvering, often when the aircraft is near

stalling speed. Sometimes pilots have to punch out of aircraft sitting dead still on a taxyway, or (as famous Russian test pilot Anatoly Kvotcher did at the Paris Air Show in 1989) from a jet almost inverted, with no forward airspeed, a couple of hundred feet off the deck.

Proper seat function depends on three factors: altitude, airspeed, and attitude. When the pilot starts the ejection sequence there must be enough altitude (and time) for the canopy to separate, for the seat to fire, and for the guidance system (if any) in the seat to correct the seat flight path away from the ground. If you happen to be inverted and 50 feet above the ground when the engine quits, don't pull that yellow ring just yet - you'll be rocketed into the terrain by the seat. Use whatever airspeed may be left to roll right side up, then depart. Sensors in the seat control when and where the parachute deploys.

Most problems with ejections happen down close to the deck, at low or very low altitude. Just what constitutes low altitude depends on the aircraft; if you happen to be in an F-16 at Mach 2 and pointed straight down, "low altitude" might mean 10,000 feet above ground level (AGL). "Very low altitude" is any ejection at or below 500 feet AGL. In either case, modern seats incorporate automatic systems to minimize the risks.

A "zero-delay lanyard" attaches to the D-ring used to manually deploy the parachute. With this system, when the pilot separates from the seat (whether or not he is conscious) the parachute is automatically activated, bypassing the normal and much slower opening mechanisms. The SOP for

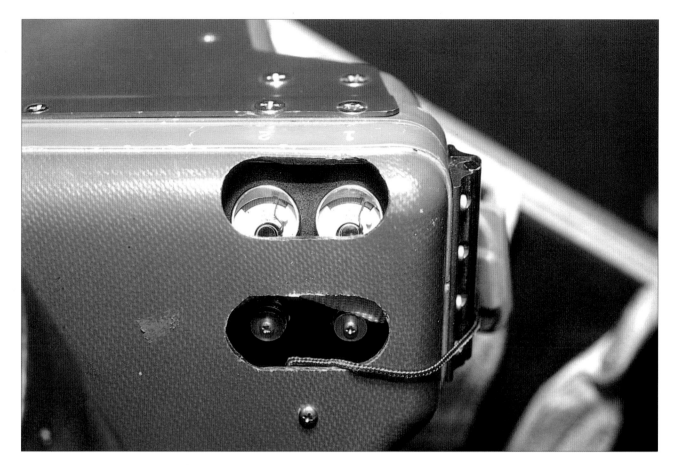

seats equipped with this feature is to attach the lanyard before take-off and disconnect it after passing through 10,000 AGL; the lanyard is re-attached at the same altitude during descent.

Another problem with ejections, particularly at low level, used to be entanglement of the deploying parachute with the seat. Nowadays a cable attached to the aircraft pays out as the seat's rocket motor blasts the pilot away from the cockpit; at about 200 feet from the aircraft this cable's travel runs out, and tension is briefly applied to the seat before it separates. This "snubber" system has the effect of stabilizing the seat's attitude and preventing some of the tumbling that would otherwise occur.

A lot of ejection problems at low altitude turn out to be related to the separation of the pilot from the seat assembly, an event that happens relatively slowly above 10,000 feet AGL but which must obviously take place much faster close to the ground. A one-second-delay connector on the pilot's lap belt activates below 10,000 feet - then you're forcefully booted from the seat by another system attached to the take-up reel. At just about the time when the seat reaches the end of its tether, when the buckle on the lap belt pops and you're watching the ground rushing up at you, another life-saving device actuates: the drogue gun. This system fires a small, heavy projectile which pulls the parachute canopy from its container, extends the suspension lines, and accelerates the opening process. Once the canopy is out of the container yet another system - the canopy spreader - fires several more weights, these being attached

to the skirt of the canopy. Shortly after this system fires you should feel the welcome tug of the risers on your harness; look up and inspect the canopy for burn holes or lines that have tangled, then look down at your likely landing spot. You have, as they say, cheated death again.

Even when everything works properly you can still be injured in an ejection. The opening shock is usually awful: eleven Gs are typical at 14,000 feet, but over thirty Gs are possible when the canopy deploys at Flight Level 400 (40,000 feet). You will be lucky to survive 30G; your helmet and boots may be stripped away, limbs broken, and other injuries sustained. Subsystems within the seat are designed to automatically reduce this hazard, some by allowing the seat and pilot to fall to a lower altitude before the parachute deploys, others by slowing the deployment sequence of the canopy and allowing a gradual deceleration.

If you survive the ejection and the 600-knot wind blast, and then the opening shock, you still risk a parachute malfunction. These are rare, but they do happen; panels sometimes blow out, leaving a hole; occasionally a shroud line will cross over the canopy during deployment, partially collapsing it; either of these mishaps will increase your rate of descent. The canopy design used for USAF emergency rigs is flat and circular - and subject to oscillation caused by air spilling first out of one side, then the other. You can counteract this problem by hauling down on the high-side risers, or by using the four-line release available on some parachute models. This is activated by tugging the two red nylon loops attached to the inside of the rear risers; four suspension lines release, a pair from each of the rear risers, creating a lobe on the canopy which allows a little air to escape and slowing oscillation.

All in all, blasting your way out of a fast jet is a thrill you can profitably live without; there is a wealth of real accumulated wisdom in that traditional aviator's phrase about the foolishness of leaving "a perfectly good airplane".

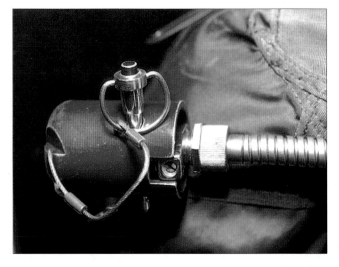

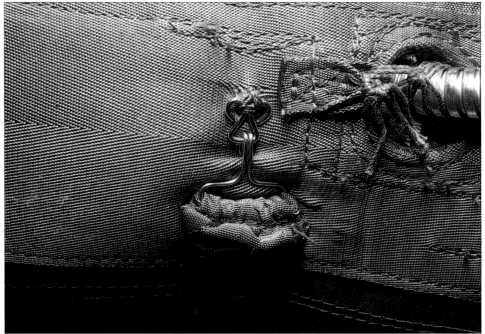

(Top right) The parachute is activated by the cable within this housing; the red cover protects the coupling when the parachute is removed from the seat assembly for inspection and maintenance.

(Right) Detail of part of the ER-2 seat parachute container - still activated, like the backpacks of 50 years ago, by hooks, eyes and elastic bands. If it works, leave it alone.

(Left) Shoulder strap attachment points, ER-2 seat.

(Above) Part of the pre-start checklist for the ER-2 pilot involves strapping on these stirrups, which will pull his feet back against the seat in the event of ejection to prevent flail injuries.

(Left) These two fittings attach to the Pilot Protective Assembly, supplying oxygen from the aircraft. In the event of a failure in the primary supply a tug on the green "apple" will activate a reserve supply.

(Left & below) Navy technicians work on a stripped-down seat from an F-14 Tomcat.(Photos Robert Genat)

(Left & below) Navy technicians work on a stripped-down seat from an F-14 Tomcat.(Photos Robert Genat)

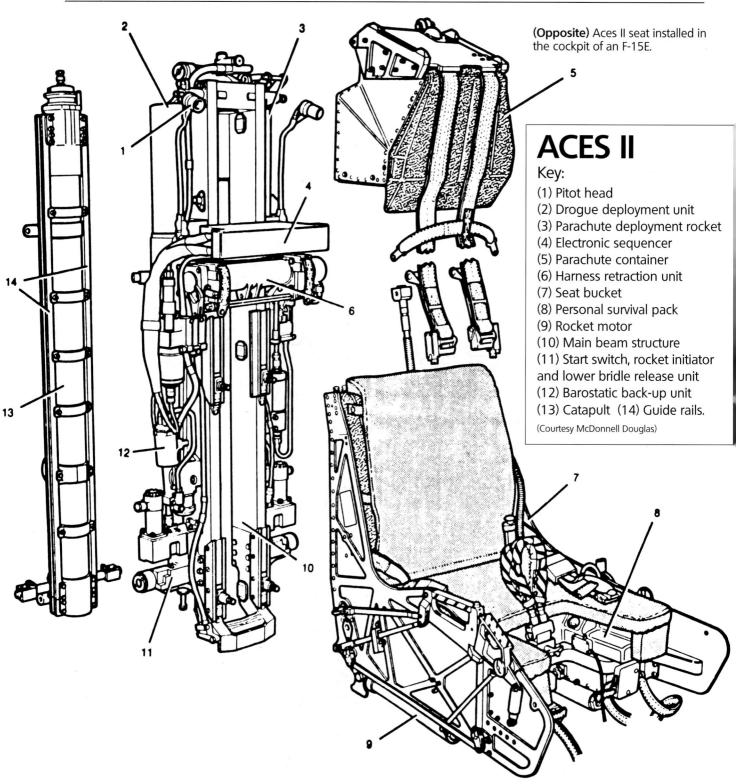

(**Opposite**) Aces II seat installed in the cockpit of an F-15E.

ACES II

Key:
(1) Pitot head
(2) Drogue deployment unit
(3) Parachute deployment rocket
(4) Electronic sequencer
(5) Parachute container
(6) Harness retraction unit
(7) Seat bucket
(8) Personal survival pack
(9) Rocket motor
(10) Main beam structure
(11) Start switch, rocket initiator and lower bridle release unit
(12) Barostatic back-up unit
(13) Catapult (14) Guide rails.

(Courtesy McDonnell Douglas)

The McDonnell Douglas ACES II (Advanced Concept Ejection Seat), chosen by the USAF as standard for the F-15, F-16, A-10, B-1B and T-46, is an extremely sophisticated device. Multiple operating modes optimize its performance depending upon the aircraft and the particular escape conditions, by means of self-contained sensors and precision-timed electronic sequencing. A gyro-controlled vernier rocket with 700lbs of vectored thrust corrects the seat attitude for high or low centre of gravity and for the particular aero forces encountered.

The typical timing sequence for ejection from an F-15 or F-16 is as follows: Rocket catapult fires; (0.17 seconds) drogue deploys; (0.18 seconds) stabilizing rocket ignites; (1.17 seconds) parachute deploys; (1.32 seconds) drogue releases from seat; (1.42 seconds) seat releases from crewman; (2.8 seconds) parachute inflates; (6.3 seconds) survival pack and liferaft deploy to hang below crewman on line. This sequence can be adjusted - for instance, the timing is set up differently for A-10 pilots, who will typically be operating at lower altitude and speed; and will be automatically interrupted if the self-contained sensors so dictate, to avoid the parachute opening too high and too quickly. A survival rate of 80 per cent is claimed for the ACES during emergency ejections; by contrast, the survival rate for aircrew who stay with their aircraft under such circumstances is around 15 per cent.

(Above) The ejection seat handles in the F-15E Strike Eagle are outboard of the pilot's knees, rather than between them as in some earlier aircraft. On the flight line they are carefully secured with guards, pins and warning flags.

(Left) Ejection seat handle in an F-16 Fighting Falcon, between pilot's knees.

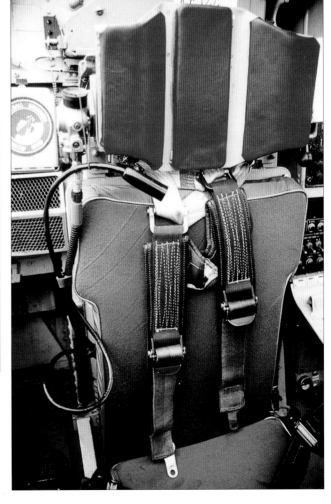

(Top, above & right) The F-111 Aardvark is the only military fixed-wing aircraft in the current USAF inventory that does not employ ejection seats. When the crew pull the handle the entire cockpit separates from the rest of the airframe and descends to earth as a capsule under a big 70-foot parachute. A large air bladder inflates beneath it to cushion the final impact somewhat, being designed to rupture in a controlled way.

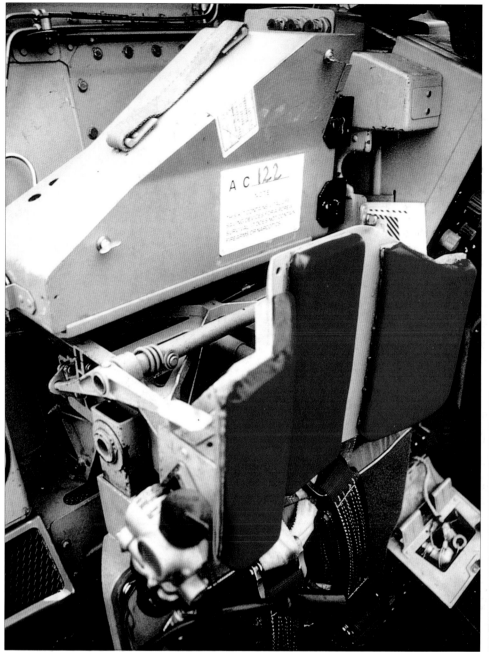

(**Left**) The F-111 crew's survival supplies are packed in the triangular metal case stowed behind the right seat; it is a sad sign of the times that the label has to warn off thieves by declaring that the kit does not contain firearms or drugs.

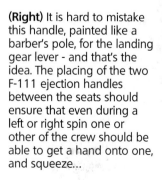

(**Right**) It is hard to mistake this handle, painted like a barber's pole, for the landing gear lever - and that's the idea. The placing of the two F-111 ejection handles between the seats should ensure that even during a left or right spin one or other of the crew should be able to get a hand onto one, and squeeze...

(Left & below) The crew of an F-111 of the 522nd TFS "FIREBALLS", 27th TFW carry out their preflight checks. Because the cockpit canopy is not jettisoned to provide a pathway for individual ejection, but has to protect the crew during the descent of their capsule, the clamshell hatches are more massively constructed and latched than the "bubbles" of other current types. Punching out of an Aardvark may be different from other ejections in many respects; but it is still painful, hazardous, disorienting, and a ride with no guaranteed happy ending.